ABOUT THE AUTHOR

Helen Kensett is a sales expert. She runs the Convince Consultancy, which helps complicated businesses in crowded markets create compelling sales and marketing campaigns. Increasingly, she is using her sales experience and keen interest in human psychology to build highly personalised digital buyer experiences. She is on a mission to enhance sales activity by using tech, not to make sellers redundant but to make them more intelligent about their approaches. This is about using technology to raise empathy, enhance customer-centricity and ultimately raise standards.

Through her brand Sales Mind, she equips national and international sales teams with the mindset and skills to sell more, more often. Clients include some of the world's most exciting and innovative technology firms, through to more established companies, including Channel 4, Google, Ogilvy, the *Telegraph* and KPMG.

ABOUT THE ILLUSTRATOR

Kat Leuzinger was born in Zurich, Switzerland, to Swiss and Japanese parents. After studying graphic design at Central St Martins, she helped establish digital agency unit9 in London, later deciding to dedicate her time fully to illustration. Kat's clients have included Kenzo Parfums, Penguin Books, GAP, Microsoft and Honda. She has collaborated with several merchandise distributors and independent luxury fashion labels throughout Europe, Australia and the USA and has participated in several international group shows and exhibitions. Kat's work has been widely recognised by international awards including D&AD, Creative Circle, The One Show, London International Awards, Cannes Cyber Lion and BIMA.

SALES MIND

48
TOOLS TO HELP
YOU SELL

....

HELEN KENSETT
ILLUSTRATED BY KAT LEUZINGER

....

P

PROFILE BOOKS

For Emily, Hannah and Gracie. My best work.

. . . .

First published in Great Britain in 2016 by
Profile Books Ltd
3 Holford Yard
Bevin Way
London
WC1X 9HD
www.profilebooks.com

A CIP catalogue record for this book is available from the
British Library.

ISBN: 978 1 78125 631 2
eISBN: 978 1 78283 245 4

Illustrations by Kat Leuzinger
Text design by Matt Wilson

Printed and bound in Great Britain by Clays, Bungay, Suffolk

The paper this book is printed on is certified by the © 1996 Forest
Stewardship Council A.C. (FSC). It is ancient-forest friendly. The
printer holds FSC chain of custody SGS-COC-2061

CONTENTS

THE 48 TOOLS

THE SELLER MINDSHIFT

TO SEE

TO THINK: SYNTHESISING YOUR SELL

TO THINK: COMMUNICATING YOUR SELL

TO IMPROVE

CLOSING THE SALE

PART I:

THE GROUNDWORK

eat *Your*

ales *Mind*'

'SO JOIN THE NEW REVOLUTION
TO FREE THE BATTERY HUMAN
'CAUSE WE WERE BORN TO BE
FREE RANGE.'
STORNOWAY

The sales profession has changed beyond recognition and even experienced sellers, yet to catch up, are failing to close the sale.

What are they doing wrong?

More crucially, what should they be doing right? Is there a secret which sets the rapidly decreasing number of successful sellers apart from the rest?

Yes, there is. And this book sets out the formula. It's something the best sellers have always known.

The Shift from Techniques ...

There's no shortage of guidance available on how to succeed at sales. Bookshops and blogs are brimming with advice which promises that, with application, we'll move our unsuspecting prospects from cold to sold. Whether we're selling software, advertising or expertise, there's a plethora of tried and tested techniques setting out what to say, where to say it and how often.

But we live in a climate where buyers are tired of clichéd techniques; in a complex, competitive, budget-tight market where buyers have more than enough of what we're all selling; in a sales environment where one day they're picking up the phone, and the next defaulting to voicemail; in a market where being struck by lightning is more likely than a response to a sales email. In a market like this, a market just like the one we're experiencing today, outdated techniques won't work. We can't hang our hat on these techniques alone and still expect to deliver. The challenging reality for sellers is that the more we try to push for the sale in the traditional sense, across outdated media, the quicker we fail.

... to Mastery of Your Sales Mind
In today's challenging environment, one thing above all others is keeping the successful sales professional buoyant: mastery of their sales mind.

Surprising as it may be, all of us possess the mental software to deliver on any conceivable sales challenge we face. We are all furnished with an inbuilt, inherent range of mental mechanisms which translate into the right skills we need in order to achieve almost any sales task we set our minds to. To master your sales mind, you must perfect these natural human skills for selling.

But that's just half of the battle. Whilst these are inherent skills, accessing and utilising them still takes effort. As we'll discover, there are many obstacles in the path of true sales success and achieving it has become increasingly challenging. Our innate ability to sell our wares has been clouded by the life we live today. And it's not getting easier.

One of the biggest challenges we all face is dealing with the overwhelming volume of information we receive. We're distracted and often default decisions to autopilot. With our minds in this mode it is almost impossible to make an impact. In this mental state, we're effectively asleep on the job.

It's unsurprising, then, that many sales approaches are failing to produce what's required in order to secure the sale. Failure in sales today is not due to a lack of experience or even a lack of confidence, but increasingly down to an inefficient sales mind.

This book provides an account of how to understand and master the most amazing apparatus at your disposal: your very own sales mind.

AN ENTIRE SKILL

When we examine sales activity across different markets and products, it is enlightening to discover that selling can be described as an 'entire' skill. An entire skill is something which, to the untrained eye, appears to be a single skill (like fishing or drawing), but which can actually be divided into simpler, more manageable steps, each of which can be mastered separately.

The three uniquely human mental skills which make up the entire skill of selling are: **to see**, **to think** and **to improve**. We must perfect these three skills in order to deliver an effective sale.

These distinct skills can be mastered individually and combined to make selling more accessible to us all. By breaking down the entire, seemingly opaque skill of sales, we make explaining how to do it, and – more importantly – actually doing it, much more straightforward. Once you have learnt this entire skill, you can then use and improve it for life.

Skill 1: To See

We are all observing machines, built with a natural mental toolkit for sight that has helped keep humans at the top of the food chain for generations.

But using our ability **to see** in order to sell involves much more than just a rapid response to a visual stimulus. First, it involves the active process of seeing all the materials available to us, using our innate abilities to see the absolute truth in the situation that confronts us. This includes your buyer's complete reality, which is not static but in flux, changing constantly, and every detail about your product and offer.

This is complemented by a passive process: the use of our intuitive psychology, our intuition, to predict our buyers' behaviour. It took millions of years for us to develop the psychology we have today and a million more will have to pass for this to vary even slightly. As sellers, an awareness of this unchanging human nature – and specifically the way it relates to the desires and decision-making processes of our target audience – is a key component in being able **to see**.

ENTIRE SKILL

IMPROVE
THINK
SEE

Active seeing and passive intuition, applied together, enable us to acquire the right knowledge and see the complete picture. This is the first step in all sales activity.

Skill 2: To Think

The second skill of the entire is **to think**. In other words, to use the knowledge acquired from Skill 1 and to extract the facts that matter for your specific buyer audience. **To think** also means analysing the problem and recognising which bits of your knowledge will answer it. This involves using our innate mental capacity for pattern recognition, to create links between seemingly unrelated bits of information. This skill is motivated by our Instinct to unravel and simplify something more complex.

Essentially, **to think** is being able to recognise exactly what's relevant and exciting about your offer and to recombine and reshape this into relevant and compelling sales communication for your target audience.

Skill 3: To Improve

The final skill of the three is **to improve**. You need to pursue the sell, make mistakes along the way and even fail. If this happens, you need to be flexible – learn, rethink and use the experience to innovate and up the creative ante, adding all-important impact to your selling.

To improve effectively is to embrace the fact that sales success is a process and the best, most impactful ideas take time, practice – and several attempts. Very few, if any, successful sales endeavours follow a straight path to success.

Embracing this process-based approach is the essence of great improving. And this flexible skill, propelled by a desire always to be learning, builds your sales excellence. Being aware of this process, and comfortable with it, marks out the best sales minds.

The subject and circumstances of each sales activity will vary, of course, but how we recognise and develop each skill is the real measure of long-term sales success. Whatever we're selling, we can learn to extract and perfect these key skills. And the more frequently we use them, the more automatic they will become.

Race Against the Machine

The great race for sellers has always been against competitors. How do we innovate, excite and win customers faster than them? But in recent years, as technology has developed, machines – or more accurately, clever algorithms – have been increasingly deployed to perform activities previously reserved for the human brain.

Does this suggest that pressure in sales today does not come just from hungry competitors, but that a race is raging against clever technologies too? Is technology coming to take over our sales and marketing jobs?

Graeme Codrington, futurist at global consultancy TomorrowToday, warns in a *Fast Company* interview that 'some of the hottest jobs of today could be obsolete by 2025'. And Ray Kurzweil, chief of innovation for Google, in his eye-opening book *How to Create a Mind: The Secret of Human Thought Revealed*, agrees: 'There are hundreds of tasks and activities formerly the sole province of human intelligence that can now be conducted by computers, usually with greater precision and at vastly greater scale.' And the projected date for the first supercomputer with the same processing power as the human brain is 2020.

We've all experienced the reality that few tasks are safe from increasingly human-like algorithms. Researching leads, data collection, vast-scale analysis, real-time measurement: all these sales activities and many more are now carried out with little human input. So why, then, are we bothering to master these skills at all when in a few years they'll be obsolete?

Because the processing power of these technologies does not necessarily represent functionality. Whilst the working speed, efficiency and breadth of these tools in many cases far exceed those of the human brain, when it comes to truly intelligent activities they are no way near as advanced.

Cognitive-psychology expert Steven Pinker notes in his book *The Language Instinct* that 'the main lesson of thirty-five years of AI (artificial intelligence) research is that hard problems are easy and easy problems are hard. The mental abilities of a four year old that we take for granted – recognising a face, lifting a pencil, walking across a room, answering a question – in fact solve some of the hardest engineering problems ever conceived.'

For centuries people have been scared that machines will overpower us, but it has not happened yet. It's all too easy to give computers more credit than they deserve.

Think again about the entire skill of selling: our innate mental algorithms that translate into the three key sales skills are extremely simple and, as we'll discover, are uniquely human. These ingeniously engineered mental skills are the foundation of every great sales mind and will be as powerful in one hundred years as they are now.

Learning to master these skills will ensure your selling transcends this rapid technological change.

HOW TO USE THIS BOOK

I have been fortunate enough during my career in sales, and more recently with my sales consultancy, to have sold across almost every sector – from fast-paced media companies to complicated technology firms to traditional financial services. Over the course of this long career, I have experienced each skill of the entire: seeing, thinking and improving, leading to the ultimate goal of closing the sale. Regardless of sector or buyer, these core skills remain constant requirements for every successful sale.

To help you master each of these individual skills, and eventually combine them for a successful sale, I have organised the book into chapters for each core skill, prefaced by the important mindful groundwork needed before you start, and followed by that crucial moment of closing the sale at the end.

Along the way, you'll encounter forty-eight practical tools, each one represented and reinforced by an illustration, which walk you through the secrets of truly great selling and help you develop the skills and the sales mind for it. Whatever you're selling, however crowded, complicated or competitive the market, these tools will hone your thinking, and ensure you are one step ahead of the rest.

They will help you:
- become more focused, and develop a mindful approach to selling – **The Seller Mindshift** *(Chapter 3)*
- gather crucial knowledge of your buyer, market and product – **To See** *(Chapter 4)*
- identify the relevant aspects of your information and communicate them clearly – **To Think** *(Chapter 5)*
- embrace the process of ongoing learning and up your creativity – **To Improve** *(Chapter 6)*
- identify how to clinch the deal – **Closing the Sale** *(Chapter 7)*.

These tools are methods and not answers. You could learn the theory with limited long-term effect, but for the best results you should apply the techniques in your own sales scenarios, incorporating these new approaches into your day-to-day selling, and learning from your own mistakes. This is what the tools are designed to help you do.

The book is designed for you to dip in and out of, selecting tools that are relevant for you in the moment, or skills that you'd like to build on for the future. You can choose to never read the book from cover to cover, or to fill it with Post-it notes and marginalia.

Part II, The Tools, is the 'meat' of the book, but before you get started on it, you might choose to read Chapter 2, The Brain: A Seller's Guide. The tools themselves often refer to the different parts of our brain, its left and right sides, our conscious and unconscious psychology, and all these things are explained in this chapter. So if you ever find yourself wondering what the 'Feeler' is, or what 'gut reactions' have to do with selling, then this is the place to turn to for answers.

As well as decoding the evolution of our brain and its relationship to sales, I have also drawn on philosophy, cognitive psychology and modern neuroscience to develop tools that situate sales within a broader cultural context, providing answers beyond business-to-business sales questions. With their emphasis on developing your innate skills, the tools will also be useful in your personal life, in any situation where you want to observe, analyse, improve and persuade more effectively.

By the end of the book, you will have mastered your sales mind and be ready to revolutionise your selling in every context. Great selling starts with you.

THIS IS
ALL ABOUT
YOU!!

2

'THE PRINCIPLES OF PSYCHOLOGY
ARE FIXED AND ENDURING.
YOU WILL NEVER NEED TO
UNLEARN WHAT YOU LEARN
ABOUT THEM.' CLAUDE C. HOPKINS

In this chapter you will:

- **get to grips with the basic workings of the brain and how the relevant functions impact on our psychology to create our mind**

- **be introduced to the Feeler and the Thinker, which produce, respectively, fast and slow thinking**

- **understand why and how our sales mind, and in turn our entire skill, is increasingly challenged.**

To get to grips with mastering each crucial sales skill, and in turn our sales mind, we must first examine our standard equipment: the brain. In understanding its physical properties, you will better understand the mind – the non-physical element that creates our behaviour, personality and attitudes, and shapes our psychology. As Pinker clarifies: 'the mind is not the brain but what the brain does'.

THE KLUDGE

It is widely accepted that the brain we have today – its structures, features, and processes – has been shaped by natural selection over hundreds of millions of years, and that much of its basic set-up hasn't changed since we were hunter-gatherers. Our daily life may have changed dramatically – we are no longer searching for food or outwitting prey to ensure species survival – but our brain's essential structures and processes have remained constant. This makes it incredibly effective at certain skills, like spotting prey and problem-solving, and less effective at others, like dealing with the information we consume today in alarming volumes.

In his aptly named book *The Accidental Mind*, David Linden, Professor of Neuroscience at Johns Hopkins University, describes the brain as 'an organ built out of yesterday's parts ... The brain is what engineers would call a "kludge". It's a clumsy design inelegantly constructed but none the less gets the job done.'

This is the tool we have at our disposal, to understand, use and conquer. It may be an old kludge but, as with any piece of machinery, it will perform better if we understand and exploit its particularities.

So let's examine those particularities in more detail.

THE JOURNEY TO THE MODERN MIND

Around 500 million years ago, the journey to the mind we have today began when nerve cells, or neurons, started to extend and organise themselves into distinct systems with distinct functions – some controlled sight, some smell, some sound. This was the first, primitive brain, located at the back of the skull at the top of vertebrates' spines. Its simple structure enabled vertebrates to process basic emotions associated with species survival.

To allow us to react to even more stimulus from our environment, on top of this brain a system of structures known as the limbic system developed, which enabled more complex emotional processing. Another crucial structure, the hippocampus, developed here and formed our associative and long-term memory system, which has a colossal capacity. This explains why emotional memories tend to linger – especially negative ones. These structures are the biggest contributor to our intuitive psychology, or instinct.

The early primitive systems within this region evoke and provoke, respond and react to emotional stimuli, so I'll refer to this area of the brain as our Feeler.

Information entering the brain through our senses (sight, smell, taste, touch and sound) flows first to the Feeler, along connections between the neurons, or neural pathways. These connections across the Feeler aren't particularly complex and this results in extremely fast reactions and instant feelings, which we're not always aware we're having.

These reactions are described as unconscious and manifest themselves as gut reactions and instincts. But they nevertheless have a significant impact on our behaviour. We can all relate to the sense that something just doesn't *feel* right or, more pertinently, when you're being pitched something, the feeling that you can't relate to the seller or approach. This gut feeling has a strong influence on you, but you can't necessarily explain why.

Our Feeler is not alone in making our decisions. Due to big changes in our wider physical environment, the brain experienced a further rapid expansion in size and a region called the cerebral cortex expanded forward into our skull. This is the most recognisable part of the brain, surrounded by wrinkly grey tissue and divided into two symmetrical sides that give the brain its walnut shape. This structure allowed the maximum volume of brain to fit into our tight skulls.

In contrast to the Feeler, the neurons in this front region are densely connected and each individual neuron connects to billions of others. Neurons here continuously pass information between each other; their connectivity results in what is known as consciousness. Unlike with our Feeler, we're aware of making the decisions that stem from the cerebral cortex.

This neural set-up fosters our intellectual abilities and the more rational processing of information. It's this mind that decides what to do with incoming information and doesn't simply react. And it's this mind and this higher-level thinking that makes us uniquely human.

I'll refer to this area of our brain as our Thinker. Within the Thinker a process known in cognitive psychology as 'neural computation' takes place. This is the idea that the brain processes information like a computer. The Thinker doesn't react rapidly to information like the Feeler, but computes it, attempts to make sense of it and binds it together into a single coherent picture.

Across the Thinker there is a relatively fixed grid pattern of connectivity created by criss-crossing ropes of neural pathways. The huge number of connections between neurons means the Thinker loves deciphering patterns and searching for meaning. The Thinker is a meaning-making machine and the process of finding meaning is called our working memory: the process of holding thoughts in our mind long enough to enable a pattern to be found, and for these thoughts to be manipulated as required.

It's this process of pattern recognition that is responsible for our ideas and our ability to think 'what if...', 'if...then...', and land on the insight. The longer the thoughts are, the more time and space they have to be manipulated and combined with information stored in our long-term memory and intuitive psychology – and the more likely we're going to stumble across the right insight and solve the problem in hand. Long thoughts are the key here.

As early as 415 BC, Socrates, the great Greek philosopher and founding father of Western philosophy, maintained that the product of thought – i.e. that which stems from the Thinker – is superior to the product of intuition – our Feeler's gut response.

Long Thought...

Bingo

LEFT AND RIGHT

To add further to the complexity, the Thinker is split down the middle into two symmetrical regions, the left and the right hemispheres.

While it's difficult to pinpoint precisely where all activity is happening within the brain, as it's so marvellously complex, brain imaging does reveal that the two sides have different ways of operating and a quite distinct functionality.

The main differences that have been identified are the left brain's slant towards a more analytical, precise and time-sensitive approach, with a focus on detail and depth. It's also associated with language. In comparison, the right brain processes things in a holistic way rather than breaking them down, likes the big picture, and is more involved in visual perception than in language.

This division of labour between the two sides can be attributed to the fact that the neural pathways in the right hemisphere tend to be longer than in the left, and connect neurons that are in fact further away. This suggests that the right brain is better at drawing on several brain areas at a time, including our Feeler and its mass of unconscious information. This neural set-up therefore favours lateral thinking, big-picture thinking and artistic activities. In contrast, in the left brain, the neurons are more densely connected and this explains why it is better equipped to do more intense, detailed work.

Most recent arguments focus on the powerful uses of both sides of the Thinker, as Chris McManus explains in his book *Right Hand, Left Hand*: 'the left hemisphere knows how to handle logic and the right hemisphere knows about the world. Put the two together and one gets a powerful thinking machine.'

FAST AND SLOW

More neural connections run up from the Feeler to the Thinker and, as such, more information flows upwards than the other way around. When responding to external stimuli, the information flows first to the Feeler; the wiring in the brain thus favours the Feeler's emotional, unconscious gut reaction.

In the forest or on the plains millions of years ago, the Feeler would have instantly decided if something was life-threatening, and any fear would have provoked an immediate fight-or-flight reaction.

If, on the other hand, the information or object was in fact life-preserving or particularly alluring, it was passed forward for further examination.

Most psychologists now agree that our brains operate on this two-system basis. Daniel Kahneman, in his bestselling book *Thinking, Fast and Slow*, describes how our brain is split into two systems, and how all mental life can be represented by the metaphor of two agents: 'System 1' and 'System 2', which produce, respectively, fast and slow thinking. These are the equivalent of what I have called the Feeler and the Thinker.

According to Kahneman, because System 1 is fast, it's the secret boss of many decisions. System 2, on the other hand, likes to lurk in the background, stepping in if completely necessary. It's much slower and more logical but also much more cognitively exhausting. It's System 1 that's in charge.

All information entering the brain defaults to System 1, or the Feeler, which decides to run or hide, kill or kiss, yes or no – then only if necessary does the information get passed to System 2, the Thinker, for a more detailed and rational examination. All of our decision-making, whether deciding to retreat to the cave or delete a sales approach, follows this default pattern.

Today, with so much information to calculate, your buyer's Feeler, their gut reaction, will cause them to delete your sales approach before the Thinker, the conscious mind, even gets involved.

STRENGTHS AND WEAKNESSES

Using the Thinker and our working memory does come with limitations. According to cognitive psychologist George Miller in his highly cited 1956 paper, 'one can only hold seven items plus or minus two in the conscious working memory'. And recent research puts this closer to three to five things. The Thinker tends to get overwhelmed easily.

Conversely, the Feeler can store a huge volume of information, and accounts for 85 per cent of our overall thinking. Its influence cannot be ignored.

Recent research suggests that we never forget an experience – it's just stored in our long-term, associative memory. This makes the Feeler an incredibly powerful source of innate creative stimulus that goes with us wherever we go. And this enormous capacity for storage is brilliant at completing tasks where many variables are involved. But we have to know how to access it. We'll examine this in Chapter 6 'To Improve'.

THE CHALLENGED MIND

So what does this all mean for our sales mind? Well, we're all – buyers and sellers alike – equipped with the same mental mechanisms that dictate our thought processing and decision-making. And this kludge is what we take with us into the world of buying and selling, a world that is increasingly complex and full of distractions. The proliferation of technology is, of course, a big part of this.

Take the next working generation: the eighteen to twenty-four year olds. Of this demographic, 84 per cent have a smartphone in their pocket, which changes how they approach almost every activity they're faced with. Your buyers are all operating in this burgeoning world of smart digital tools that support (and control) their lives.

A major side effect of this rapid adoption of technology is information overload. We have seen and are continuing to experience a mammoth growth in the information available to (and forced on) us all. Plus we're often juggling several things at once: multiple projects, calls, Twitter, Facebook and emails – and that's just work-related. On top of this, our social life is now clamouring for our online attention twenty-four hours a day. Friends, family, the media, brands we actively follow – all are seeking our attention and we're in constant overdrive.

It is crucial to understand the implications for our sensitive, delicate minds.

THE THINKER OVERLOADED

Due to the sheer amount of cognitive energy used by our Thinker just carrying out our daily lives, it is designed not to pay attention all of the time. Sapping more energy than any other bodily organ, the Thinker is designed to wander: our default Thinker mode is to flutter like a butterfly, switching between attention and distraction all day long.

Recent research from Harvard suggests we spend as much as 50 per cent of our day mind-wandering, lost in a dream. This is our resting state – as the founder of modern psychology, William James, noted in 1907: 'compared with what we ought to be, we are only half awake'.

This is not surprising, and is even truer today, when we are surrounded by a myriad of distractions. It can't entirely be blamed on external stimuli, however; French psychiatrist Christophe André warns that our mind is already predisposed to distraction and fragmentation: 'It is drawn to things that are noisy or easy, just as our taste buds are drawn to things that are sweet or salty.' We are naturally drawn to easy distractions – the rustle in the library, the flicker of someone passing the office door, the buzz of a phone with a quick little admin task – as relief from intense mental exercise or sustained work on a single project. Only the most disciplined of minds are able to focus for extended periods of time and, even then, if a distraction doesn't present itself at some point, we are just as likely to make our own.

In 2007, Gloria Mark, a professor of informatics at the University of California, co-authored a study called 'The Cost of Interrupted Work: More Speed and Stress', which found that people were as likely to self-interrupt as to be interrupted by someone else. During

THE THINKER	The Feeler
SLOW	FAST
RATIONAL	EMOTIONAL
COGNITIVELY EXHAUSTING	GUT REACTION
REASONED	INSTINCTUAL
CONSCIOUS	UNCONSCIOUS
WILL TO LEARN	WILL TO LIVE
WORKING MEMORY	INTUITION
LONG THOUGHTS	QUICK REACTIONS
LOGIC	FEAR
PATTERN RECOGNITION	NO PATTERNS
OVERWHELMED EASILY	HUGE CAPACITY FOR STORAGE

the study, Mark observed people working, and saw that 'after every twelve minutes or so, for no apparent reason, someone working on a document [would] turn and call someone or email'. Mark makes the somewhat obvious argument that this behaviour is 'bad for innovation' because 'ten and a half minutes on one project is not enough time to think in-depth about anything'.

Making the most of the essential processes of our Thinker, therefore, is not easy. Even on a good day, let alone on a day filled with multiple tasks, technology and methods of communication provide constant distraction. In this climate, it's far easier to default to our fast and more efficient Feeler to make the myriad choices we face.

The Impact on Your Buyer

Our modern buyers can, therefore, be defined by the mantra 'too much information', constantly connected to their devices and experiencing multiple attempts to gain their attention from various media. In this scenario their attentional resources are simply spread too thin.

Bruce Daisley, Vice President of Direct Sales for Europe at Twitter, told me that he receives a staggering five hundred emails (still the major medium of choice for sellers) every single day, all requiring his attention. This volume of information, coming through on email alone, is enough to make any mind switch off from the majority of messages clamouring for a response – and shift mental focus only to the absolutely crucial.

This overload presents a serious challenge for sellers. Our buyers no longer feel they have the cognitive space to pay attention, resulting in a rapidly decreasing interval between buyer receptiveness (when they're open to what we're selling) and total closure (when they have closed their mind to us completely). The time available to sellers is shrinking ... fast. We don't get very long to excite any more.

This always-on, connected culture is not reserved for the workplace – we're not shutting down at home any more either. Digital strategist

Tom Chatfield calls this 'intimate computing'. Our devices have become part of us, a tool to support our lives, and, because of this, we're not tolerant of unwanted messages clogging personal inboxes and depleting device memories.

In this climate, to save time and mental energy, buyers are defaulting to their Feeler most of the time and making gut-reaction decisions based on limited information.

Mastering how to excite the Feeler is essential knowledge, then, for any sales person.

The Impact on You

And this information explosion isn't helping you develop the innate skills so necessary for efficient and successful selling. This is not the easiest time for sellers.

Just as our buyers are inundated with information, so are we, from every angle. Today's sales role typically consists of multiple tasks and masses of communication.

It's in this environment that we need to conquer our entire skill – **to see**, **to think** and **to improve**. But the problem is, this climate disturbs our mind's ideal equilibrium and we're failing to deliver.

According to Christophe André, too much or too little of anything makes us sick, and today we have too much noise and not enough down time – which makes us deficient in effective and efficient thinking. André claims that 'we have forgotten how to think as the noise, the tumult, the external racket has prevented us'. Our Thinker brains are overloaded, and we are constantly distracted.

THE DANGER ZONE

When we're attempting to solve a sales challenge, our Thinker is processing lots of information simultaneously. Nilli Lavie, Professor of Psychology and Brain Sciences at UCL, claims that it's in this mental environment that we are most likely to struggle with focus. Lavie has studied attention for decades and claims that 'if you are working in an environment of high mental load then you're more likely to be distracted'. Lavie's work has revealed that 'like any logical information-processing machine, if the brain doesn't have quite enough information to deal with, if it isn't full, it will want to fill up and will suck in any kind of distraction'.

When you're attempting to solve a sales challenge with your mind semi-loaded, you are in the focus danger zone, in danger of sucking up any old distraction and throwing your thinking off course in an instant. You will lose your train of thought, breaking off your long thoughts, drifting to a completely unrelated topic and not allowing yourself time to land on the right insight.

This natural tendency towards distraction leads to what is popularly referred to as 'mindlessness'. For social psychologist Ellen Langer, it is characterised by 'entrapment in old categories; by automatic behaviour that precludes attending to new signals; and by action that operates from a single perspective'. In other words, we are trapped in the automatic responses dictated by our Feeler.

This problem is not easily solved. In our current society and workplace culture, multitasking is encouraged and our brains are on a constant drip feed. Even the most alert of us are suffering what Langer calls 'continuous partial attention'.

This mindless approach is catastrophic for sales success; with our minds on autopilot, we fail to notice what's important. In this state, it's impossible to master our entire skill. Developing your sales mind must begin with rediscovering a mindful attention.

PART II:
THE TOOLS

'The
M

Seller
ndshift'

THE MORE I THINK ABOUT THE
QUESTION, THE MORE I AM
CONVINCED THAT LIFE IS FROM
ONE END TO THE OTHER A
PHENOMENON OF ATTENTION. '
HENRI BERGSON

The tools in this section will help you:

- *understand the crucial role of attention in mastering your sales mind*

- *recognise the difference between attention and inattention, and how to improve the former*

- *learn to focus your mind, and apply mindfulness to your selling.*

Learning to control your attention is one of the most crucial things you can do; every skill in successful selling requires focused attention. Controlling your Thinker will determine what you pay attention to and how you think effectively, by allowing you to develop long thoughts. In this way, it also enables you to embrace creative improvement. We've all heard the expression 'to have presence of mind'. **To see**, **to think** and **to improve** effectively, and in turn to sell well, we need to shift mental gear to a 'switched-on mind'.

Certain types of distraction are certainly important for elements of the creative process, and we'll examine this in Chapter 6, To Improve. But for rigour, accuracy and productivity, a razor-like focus is essential.

Nilli Lavie defines attention as having your mental resources 'concentrated on the right proportion of the information you are facing, according to your priorities'. A crucial step in mastering the ability to focus is to figure out what your priorities are; you can then move yourself from seeing everything but noticing nothing to becoming exquisitely alert. What is important here is that you're in the moment. You're seeing what is in front of you – not what you're told is there or what you think is there, but what is actually there.

We've discussed Ellen Langer's definition of 'mindlessness' and how it affects our behaviour and leads to mental laziness. On the other hand, she describes 'mindfulness' as being completely alert and awake, intentionally paying attention: 'it involves stopping to make contact with the ever-shifting experience that we are having at the time, and to observe the nature of our relationship with that experience, the nature of our presence in that moment.'

This concept of 'being mindful' has its roots in Buddhist philosophy, but is not just for monks in robes, chanting; mindfulness meditation has become extremely popular over recent years – unsurprising, given that it's proving very effective in redirecting irrelevant and distracting thoughts, and in sharpening up the Thinker. Mindfulness meditation is a very effective mental exercise designed to clear your mind. And it's this quiet and clear mind that you need in order to pay attention, a critical skill for everyday selling.

Mindful thinking helps us avoid automatic judgements and ensures we're making decisions with what Langer calls 'our most aware selves'– essential if we want to make any impact whatsoever. Success in sales belongs to the sellers who're widest awake and who find time and space to focus, giving their selling the attention it deserves.

At the centre of mindfulness is the idea of attentional control. In selling this is the first step that enables you to achieve your larger goal.

Michael Michalko, creativity expert, argues that anyone can learn to pay attention. As an exercise to prove his point, he suggests selecting a colour at random and spending the entire day looking for items of that colour. In doing so, he argues, you will suddenly discover an incredible number of objects of that colour in your daily life: 'familiar objects will become new again', he claims. By tuning in to one colour and tuning out others, you will understand that colour more deeply, your perspective will have changed. You will have allowed yourself to be mindful.

No one has yet discovered the ultimate secret to paying attention. If they had they'd be very wealthy indeed. There are no shortcuts but there are activities which can help enormously. The following four tools help sharpen up your focus, maximise the productivity of your Thinker and thus get your brain in gear for the **seller mindshift**.

CURRENT

Focus APPLY

TOOL 1: STRENGTHEN THE MIND

Just knowing it's not easy to control your wandering mind is a great step in learning to focus. Focused thinking is a mental shift and, as such, hard work – acknowledging this will ensure that you are prepared, and less likely to give up when you find your attention slipping.

Focus APPLY

IDEAL

The trick is to get to know what it feels like to be in a different state of mind from your usual energy-saving, butterfly mode of thinking – to will to be in this focused mode and to prepare for it. Start by building up a habit of clear thinking and learning what it feels like to nurture longer thoughts that aren't broken off by distraction or fickle attention.

Exercises to help you experience this mode of focused thinking – from yoga to table-top Zen gardens – are popping up everywhere, but one in particular has surged in popularity over recent months due to its mindful benefits: colouring-in for adults. From this perspective, colouring is all about regaining mindfulness and getting a break from distractions.

Mandalas are a great symbol to colour, as they are an ancient form of meditative art that draws your eye towards the centre and in doing so helps to centre the mind. Concentrating on the image whilst recognising and dispelling intrusive thoughts that enter your mind, along with the repetitive action of colouring, focuses your brain on the present. Many people who have a difficult time with more involved meditation can find this type of exercise appealing.

The more you carry out mindful activities like colouring and learn to dispel distractions, the stronger your mind will become at concentrating in more crucial scenarios when focus is essential.

TRY THIS:
Colour in the mandala. Focus on the physical activity of colouring – and not on what you're having for dinner or how you're going to get that new dress in your lunch break. Think instead about being focused on the shape in front of you, about being one with the activity.

When your mind starts to wander from the colouring, don't get irritated with yourself for getting distracted, just recognise the thought and gently release it – like catching a fish, examining it and throwing it back into the sea.

Then bring your mind back to the task at hand and continue colouring.

STRENGTHEN
THE
MIND

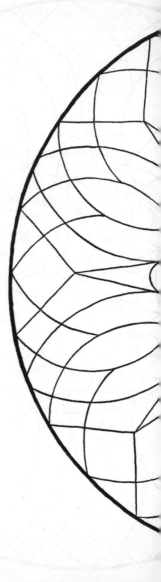

TOOL 2: DETOX THE MIND

In an article by Steve Lohr in the *New York Times* in 2007, cognitive scientist David Meyer's conclusion was clear: 'When it comes to almost any non-trivial operation, multitasking will slow you down and increase the chance of mistakes. Much research has concluded we simply don't have the capacity to divide our attention between tasks. Instead we switch rapidly between them dividing our attention into packets.'

We cannot allocate our attention to multiple things at once and expect to function at the same level as when we're just focusing on one activity. Our ability to focus reduces dramatically when overwhelmed, and when we're at all distracted, we pay attention to the wrong things.

To really have a clear picture of the task in hand, we need to give the task the individual attention it demands. Yet most often, we don't opt to shut ourselves off from distractions such as emails or texts, and don't choose to be mindful.

I'm not against technology, but it's clear that unplugging for periods is necessary for focus. By turning off unnecessary devices, you will prevent your Feeler, desperate to react emotionally to the multitude of interruptions, from breaking off your long thoughts. The most productive sellers strive to prevent their mind filling up with irrelevant media.

We need to create more of what David Allen, productivity expert and author of the bestselling book *Getting Stuff Done*, calls 'clear space'.

Unplugging completely is certainly unrealistic, and trying to close down all emails and phone calls isn't practical for hours on end. But the benefits of creating units of unplugged productivity, creating boundaries between your plugged and unplugged self, will be huge.

We must get into the habit of asking ourselves what activities we have got to do today that will be better served if we're unplugged and not spending every spare moment filling up on irrelevance. Which brings us to Tool 2.

TRY THIS:
In Tool 2, in the space in the head, list the four major distractions which prevent you having 'clear space'. Be honest with yourself here: what are your major distractions during your working day when you're trying to concentrate? Recognising these is an important step in loosening their hold on you.

There is also a nine-hour working day in Tool 2 which is divided into ninety-minute chunks. Imagine this is your working day and you have a sales challenge to conquer. Amongst all those hours, allocate yourself just ninety minutes of clear space. Mark this time in the calendar before you start the day, plan for it and stick to it. Use it to work on the challenge. This time will allow your brain to find its equilibrium and enable you to use it to its full potential.

TOOL 3: LOAD THE MIND

We've identified that our brain has a natural desire and tendency to fill up with information. When we're in this danger zone, working on a problem with our mind semi-loaded with facts, Lavie argues that rather than giving our brains *less* to do, we should give our brains *more* to

2

DETOX
THE MIND

9:00 – 10:30
10:30 – 12:00
12:00 – 13:30
13:30 – 15:00
15:00 – 16:30
16:30 – 18:00

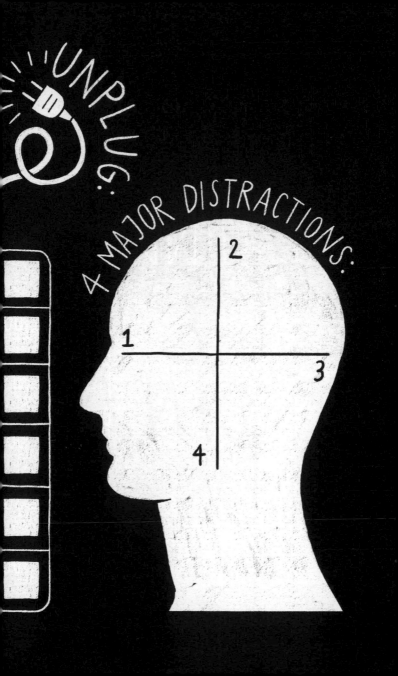

3

LOAD THE MIND

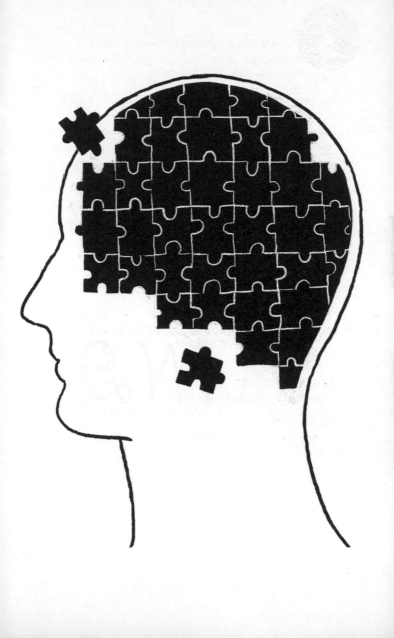

do. Her 'Load Theory' states that once the brain reaches its limit of
sensory processing – i.e. when it's full up – then it can't take anything
else in, and this includes distractions.

So when we're trying to concentrate, actually filling the mind with
relevant distractions will help you avoid the automatic influx of
irrelevant distractions. If you're awash with facts about your subject,
stacked to the limit, then you're more likely to be able to focus on it.
Relevance is key here – filling your mind with the stuff that matters.

Soft background noise can help fill your mind and focus your errant
Thinker too. Sitting in a bustling cafe, wearing headphones with no
music, can be ideal: surprisingly the gentle hum of voices keeps the
Thinker full up and in focus mode.

TRY THIS:
The trick with this tool is to work out what works for you.

*To load your mind with relevant facts, perhaps print out your current
project and lay it on the desk around you. Or write headings on Post-it
notes and place them all over your desk. You'll be visually awash with
your challenge.*

*Or perhaps find somewhere with a soft buzz of noise, not loud blaring
music but the soft patter of gentle conversation.*

*The sooner you figure out what works for you, the quicker you'll be able
to complete complex sales challenges and land on the right insight
more often.*

TOOL 4: THE PEN

As we start to recognise and apply our focused mind to the task of selling, we can think about the tool that is most crucial to both concentrating on a problem and solving it: asking questions.

Questions are at the heart of selling. We use them to see the truth of a situation, asking ourselves and others questions to make sure we don't lose sight of the most important elements, and we'll examine this in more detail in the next chapter. Crucially for us here, questions also help us to remain focused on the subject at hand, which could otherwise become blurred and confused. Using questions to identify what is significant and to stay focused is what marks out the best sellers.

To demonstrate the effectiveness of questions in keeping you focused on the matter in hand, I have adapted an exercise from the pioneering philosopher and psychologist William James.

TRY THIS:
Look at a pen on your desk and try to stay focused on it. After a while, you'll notice that either your field of vision will have become blurred so the pen is no longer crystal clear, or you are involuntarily thinking about something else altogether.

Now to the role of questions. Ask yourself questions about the pen – what colour is it? How long is it? What texture is it? How far away from you is it? How many sides does it have? Turn the answers over in your mind. By doing this you will find that you are able to keep your mind focused on the pen for longer.

This is a wonderful trick for observing the brilliance of questions in helping us remain focused.

The Pen

How long is it?

_____

What

_____

What colour is it ?

_____

naterial is it made of ?

_____

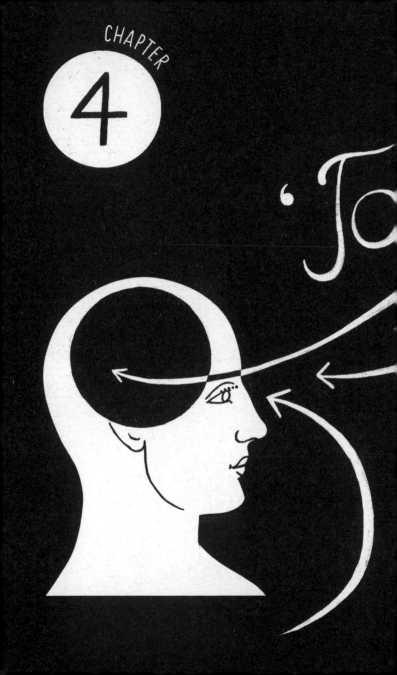

See,

'WE MUST LOVE THINGS
THAT ARE ORDINARY AND BANAL.
WE MUST OPEN OURSELVES UP
TO THE DENSITY OF THE
EVERYDAY WORLD.'

CHRISTOPHE ANDRÉ

4

Tools 5–12 will enable you to see mindfully, and to acquire knowledge of:

- *your buyer's reality, their 'now'— including their goals, challenges and future trends, both for the organisation and the individual*

- *your buyer's fixed psychology, and in particular their unconscious decision-making processes and emotional hot buttons*

- *your product, service or offer, and current and future plans to develop.*

So here we are at the beginning of what has the potential to be a flawless sales process. You're awake (hopefully) and know what focused attention feels like. Or at least you know how to prevent distractions from interrupting you when you need to be in the right frame of mind. Which brings us to the first of our core skills: **to see**.

What does 'to see' mean in practice? What do you need to see? And how are the best sellers 'seeing' differently from the rest?

To see means to understand all the raw materials of a situation, and to be completely familiar with the information that is relevant to your sell. In order to approach a sale with confidence and, eventually, to find success, you first need to see clearly the situation as it stands, and to focus on the most important elements. You must have in-depth knowledge not only of your product but also of your customer and their desires, challenges and motivations, from both an individual and organisational standpoint.

An inability to see the true reality of a situation is the biggest problem in any sale. Even experienced sellers zoom past this stage far too quickly. Time on the job doesn't necessarily correspond with better seeing. How can any of us move people and, more pertinently, get them to buy from us, if we don't know what is going on in their heads and what is influencing them?

Thomas Messett, former head of digital marketing at Microsoft Mobile, finds this type of oversight baffling: 'It's amazing how little sellers know about the industry they're selling into.'

In this chapter we take a step back, to the start of the selling process, and examine what you need to see and how to see it. The tools will help you to see your buyer's reality, understand their decision-making psychology and what will attract them to your product or offer – in other words, all a seller needs to know to make the sale.

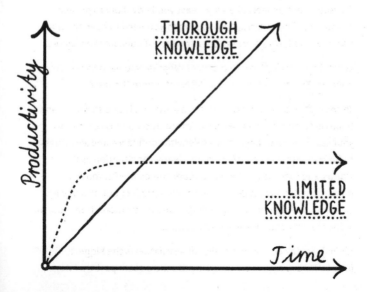

THE CRUCIAL ROLE OF KNOWLEDGE

If you think you have all the information available to you, then it's unlikely you're right. Lack of enough or the right knowledge is one of the biggest seller deficiencies.

Acquiring the right knowledge is about starting far enough back in the selling process. Many sellers outsource this collection of vital information, or wait far too long before collecting it themselves. You should be hungry to start from the word go. It's incredibly easy to fail if you don't get this bit right; more importantly, it's almost impossible to succeed.

Starting early enough in your search for information is not only key to great selling but also central to achieving great *anything*. When was the last time anyone won Wimbledon without a complete knowledge of the wonderful game? They didn't just start thinking about it when they stepped on to the court. Certainly in more recent years, professional players haven't just learnt how to hit the ball; they've learnt how the ball reacts to different surfaces; they know the skill of their opponent and the limits of their own mind. To start with limited knowledge is fatal in sport. And in sales. Particularly as in both disciplines marginal gains are the difference between winning and losing.

You can liken this knowledge to the roots of a tree. Like the foundations of knowledge, roots are what no one sees; they are ugly, not orderly and they stretch out in all directions. But they are absolutely critical – without healthy roots the tree would be restricted in the height it could reach, no matter how much the sun shone. Selling without the right knowledge will never reach great heights. Its growth potential will be limited, no matter how much you push for the sale.

TOOL 5: FOUR THINGS

So here we come to the first tool in mastering the ability **to see** effectively.

When gathering knowledge about your buyer's situation, one of the first places to start is with their central business challenges.

All industries share common frustrations dictated by the market, the competition and ongoing change. These, plus their own internal pressures, mean there are usually three or four challenges for every buyer that you can identify at any one time. They include anything from regulatory pressure to lack of enough quality talent.

Messett knows this reality only too well: 'There are three or four challenges in my mind at any one time, and if you frame yourself as the answer, you will get yourself a meeting. And it's never because you do it cheaper.'

Regardless of whether you directly solve these challenges or not, this will always be important information to gather.

TRY THIS:
Can you identify your buyers' four major pressures? What are they looking to solve? What is causing major disruption in their market, in their industry or even in their country?

It might come from inside the organisation, like motivation issues or expertise gaps, or outside, like increasing regulation. Most likely, their challenges will fall into both categories.

Once you have identified the four challenges that define your buyer's working life, write them in the spaces provided in Tool 5.

5

four
things

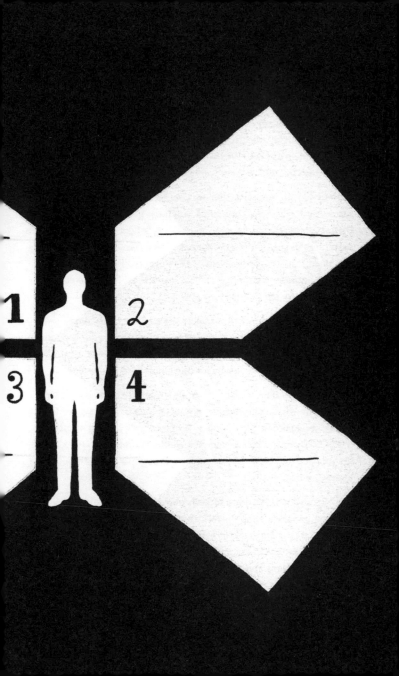

SEEING YOUR BUYER'S REALITY

Most sales training and advice starts and ends with identifying your buyer's challenges, which Tool 5 helped you to focus on. This is very important knowledge for sellers to have, but it is not enough information on its own. A friend of mine, who sells for a technology firm, summarises this by saying: 'We need to stop obsessing about problems.'

With so many options available for your buyer, all promising the same solution and the same value, you must gain a wider picture of them, beyond what everyone else is seeing. Sellers must explore their customer's big picture, the CEO's challenge, as well as their day-to-day challenges, and must perceive *who* the buyer really is. With this in mind, knowledge of your buyer's challenges must be bolstered by an Active Buyer Impression (ABI).

An ABI is a clear picture of your buyer's reality, their day-to-day experiences and goals. This reality changes regularly, is rarely clean and often complicated. Maintaining an accurate image of it is a dynamic process, which is why we call it an 'active' impression.

The ABI helps you to uncover this complex picture, and also to start focusing on what's significant. It is a set of questions, designed to enable you to see your customer's complete reality. Using questions in this way, you are forced to see the whole picture; you can no longer glance – you need to gaze, looking long enough to gain a thorough understanding.

The ABI questions force you to focus on what the other person is thinking, and are also open and inclusive, helping to get the answers you need. By thinking carefully about what you need to know and the right questions to ask, you will be able to make educated and informed decisions about the next stage of the selling process.

These are not questions to ask your buyer directly. Polling and questionnaires are great methods for collecting information about our

customers, but they don't give us the complete buyer picture we need, since our buyers can only respond to what they know. It's up to you personally as a seller to know what the buyer wants before they do. The ABI helps you to have the right information and to be that step ahead.

Writing about the brilliant advertising man Albert Lasker, David Ogilvy said that 'he combined a sense of detail with a gift for grasping the big picture, and that he had a genius for predicting the reactions of consumers'. This sums up what the ABI looks to achieve. It enables you to see the big picture, the overarching view that your right brain automatically favours, and also allows for the collection of details about the customer's day-to-day experience, thus appealing to the left brain's love of detail.

So here we come to Tools 6 and 7, the ABI. These are two central exercises in any selling activity and in many ways the most important of all forty-eight included in this book. At any given moment we need to gain an 'Active Buyer Impression'.

TOOL 6: ABI ORGANISATIONAL

The ABI Organisational is divided into eight separate questions, which give you details as well as a thorough overview of the buyer you have in mind. Tool 6 focuses on collective goals and challenges driven by the organisation.

With your buyer firmly in focus, think about the following:

1. What is their central goal?
This is vitally important. What is your buyer's primary business goal? What is their most important challenge – what keeps them awake at night? What are the big things they want to achieve?

Working with a client who was selling software to pension funds, I needed to know the answer to this question and I needed it in their language – really basic stuff, but so important. It may feel a bit silly asking something so seemingly obvious, but the answer is fundamental to the sales process. For the pension fund it was quite simply: 'realising financial return for clients whilst minimising risk'. And for another client who was selling PR services to marketing directors, the central challenge was: 'maximising exposure for the brand and increasing sales'.

These are the things that form the bedrock of your buyer's day-to-day role. These are the goals that they simply must work towards. This is their big picture. With your eye on this, you can dig for the detail, but take your eye off this and you'll be in danger of swerving off course completely.

2. What are their secondary goals?

What are the details, the day-to-day goals they need to achieve? These still create important challenges that need to be mastered, and are often the impetus for upcoming projects. These are often the executive's own challenges and goals, including departmental challenges that come with clear budget allocations.

Examples for a marketing leader could be things like:
• increasing followers on Twitter
• maximising brand awareness across Facebook
• attracting new business leads
• running a recruitment drive.

Or for a head of operations working for a hedge fund:
• enhancing transparency of reporting
• diversifying funds to improve return
• attracting more institutional investment.

3. What are their future market trends?

Every industry is evolving and has something new (and set to revolutionise current practices) on the horizon.

In reality we don't like the 'history' of something quite as much as we like the 'next big thing'. People are much more impressed by potential than by track record, and are more interested in working with a company that can propel them into the future than one that's stuck in safe mode.

The answer to this again bolsters your understanding of the buyer's big picture, and keeps your eye on the future.

4. What are their market challenges?

What is your buyer experiencing in their industry that you need to be aware of? We've covered this in Tool 5 but it's useful to repeat it here to ensure the ABI gives a complete buyer picture.

Examples of market challenges might include:
- regulatory changes
- increased demand from clients around reporting
- the move to algorithms.

5. What is their current scenario?

What is your buyer currently doing? How are they operating without you and without what you're offering? What is their status quo?

This is important in order to know where you might fit in, and how you might support and then improve their current situation.

Examples could be:
- using spreadsheets
- manually inputting data
- outsourcing
- using several different systems to complete a process.

6. What are their preconceived ideas?

What are their preconceived ideas about you and why your product would be a risky purchase? Perhaps they think your style won't fit with their brand. Or perhaps they assume you will be too expensive. Good or bad, they will definitely have their own assumptions about you and products like yours. What are they?

7. What are their anxieties in buying your product?

You must figure out what would worry your customer about buying from you – are you unknown, a risky proposition? Do they think you're going to mean a lot of extra work for them? Knowledge of their anxieties will give you the ammunition you need to reassure them in your communications.

We know from examining the brain that, most of the time, we let our gut reactions dictate our decisions. Avoiding uncertainty and danger is a central driver in this kind of decision-making. Being able to give peace of mind that your product is the sound choice is, understandably, very important.

8. What are their finite resources?

A common trait of human nature is that we tend to believe that our resources are more limited than they actually are. Ellen Langer argues we create false limits in order to share out resources, often time- or money-related, a habit again linked to our fear receptors rather than to our reason. Our buyers believe that certain resources are absolute, rather than variable.

Common limited resources include:
- time
- money
- energy
- people
- expertise.

What resources does your buyer think are limited? How could you expand these limits for them? How could you position your sell and product so that you don't overuse any single resource?

TRY THIS:
Think about and work through all the questions in the ABI Organisational. You may need to draw on advice from colleagues within your business,

6

ABI {ORGANISATIONAL}	SECONDARY G
CURRENT SCENARIO:	CENTR
PRECONCEIVED IDEAS:	FINITE RESO

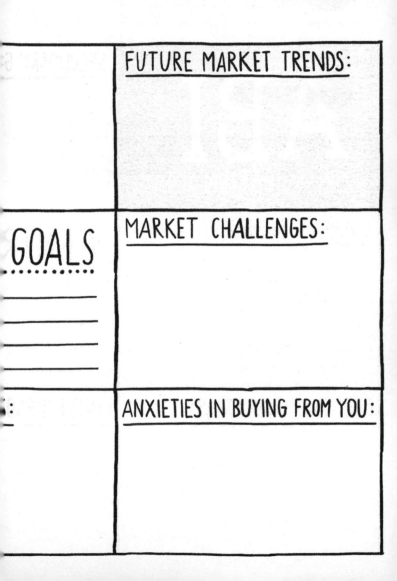

FUTURE MARKET TRENDS:

GOALS
· · · · · · · · ·
_____
_____
_____
_____

:

MARKET CHALLENGES:

ANXIETIES IN BUYING FROM YOU:

but you need to be in control of the collection of information, as you need to know all this.

Think about both the big picture and the minutiae of your customer's day-to-day experiences. If it helps, write it all down in the spaces provided in Tool 6.

TOOL 7: ABI PERSONAL

The extent of your knowledge now incorporates your buyer's organisational drivers. This is a great starting place, but you must also recognise the importance of your buyer's personal goals. This is vital for your selling, and Tool 7 looks at the goals and challenges faced by the individual buyer.

We're all human, after all, and when we're at work we are still driven by our innate human drives and desires. When we receive any form of communication, it's often our personal needs that determine our quickest reactions to the message, not our organisational needs.

Leo Burnett, renowned ad man and founder of an agency of the same name, understood this about his clients: 'I try to get a picture in my mind of the kind of people they are – how they use this product, and what it is – they don't often tell you in so many words – but what it is that actually motivates them to buy something or to interest them in something.' It is this ability to conjure the complete mental picture that separates the best sellers from the average.

Here in the ABI Personal, we are directed to think about a buyer's personal perspective. What does the individual want to achieve? What do all individuals want to achieve? What do we want – for ourselves?

You can divide your personal drivers into three principles: pleasure, progress and purpose.

Pleasure

What we're talking about here is the way your buyer's attitude is driven by a search for pleasure. Pleasure is a low-level driver and includes things like financial gain and personal praise. Surprisingly, pleasure has less of an influence on buyers than most sales messages would suggest.

Consider a sell that goes like this: 'Save time and money with our technology.'

Interesting, but ultimately undifferentiated and highly ignorable. Not only could you be one of thousands of products offering the same, non-specific benefits, but you're appealing to the short-term nature of our pleasure. The advertising industry has long sold goods on the back of pleasure claims, but this is now changing, as businesses look to move beyond such an overused technique to sell their wares. But despite its limitations and clichés, pleasure is still a useful driver to be aware of, and if you can position yourself to enhance your buyer's pleasure, you'll be moving in the right direction at least.

Progress

The essence of progress is about getting better at something: improving skills, enhancing an attribute, or moving forward with a goal or project. This is an effective driver, certainly more effective than pleasure. It's a driver I use a great deal in my own selling.

The headline for a recent client campaign taps right into this idea of progress: 'What you need to know today. To thrive tomorrow.'

This addresses the individual directly, and immediately hooks into the idea of progress. In other parts of the campaign, progress of individual members within the organisation was also addressed: 'We'll prepare your leaders for rapid and diverse developments in technology, employee demands, buyer habits, incredible competition and the evolution of marketing.' A clear progress route.

ABI {PERSONAL}

purpose

progress

pleasure

WHAT ARE YOUR BUYER'S PERSONAL GOALS?

_____
_____
_____
_____
_____
_____
_____
_____
_____
_____
_____
_____
_____
_____
_____
_____

So, ask yourself; how does your product or offer help your buyer to make progress?

Purpose

In his hierarchy of human needs, psychologist Abraham Maslow defined self-actualisation as the pinnacle of human needs. Self-actualisation means creating something ourselves – a business, a work of art, a baby, a home – and it's this experience of creation that gives our activity purpose, or meaning. A sense of meaning is hugely important in bringing us ultimate joy in life; the joy that comes from feeling that we're participating in something, not just a bystander.

Humans are meaning-making machines and we want to know that what we're doing – and, increasingly, what we're buying – has meaning. What it *means* is becoming more important than what it *does*. As sellers, we're not communicating this nearly enough.

This idea of creative ownership is even more influential than pleasure and progress in our hierarchy of personal drivers. To participate, not just stand by, can also be described as fulfilling purpose.

In its truest form, purpose at work would be the experience of the baker who rises every morning, bakes the bread and sells it in their own bakery. There is nothing closer to ultimate purpose than this. Unfortunately, in our jobs today, we often don't have the opportunity to create meaning, and many of us feel like little cogs in a big controlling wheel.

To empower your recipient with the feeling of purpose is an extremely powerful driver. Know this and use it. Are you giving them the tools to own it? Giving meaning to your sell involves making the buyer feel like they are running the bakery.

For one of my client campaigns which was highly effective at creating a sense of purpose, we developed an online tool which enabled the

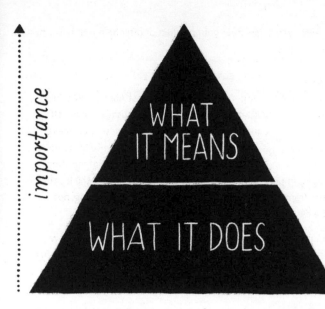

buyer to answer thirteen questions to determine their own in-house technical capability. In turn they were able to use the online tool to map their improvement journey across a five-year time frame. This was shareable, actionable and utterly practical.

Rarely does selling look beyond the lower levels of pleasure and progress, but there is huge potential for sales and marketing to feed the need for self-actualisation and make the meaning crystal clear.

TRY THIS:
Think about your buyer's personal drivers. Adding pleasure and progress should be pretty simple, but how about including purpose?

Can you give your buyer the tools to create and own the process? Or at least give them the feeling of control?

THE FULL ABI EXAMPLE

Combining the Organisational and Personal Active Buyer Impressions creates a terrific tool for gaining both a big-picture and a detailed view of your customer, without limiting your knowledge to just their problems.

Here is a working example developed for a client who offered mobile app technology to hotels. The buyers were heads of technology in the hospitality sector.

ABI Organisational

1. *Central goal*
- Expand the hotel portfolio: ten new hotels in two years.

2. *Secondary goals*
- maximise revenue per available room
- increase incremental revenue
- happy guests
- efficient procedures
- effective customer communication strategies pre, during and post stay
- the latest technology available for guests
- direct bookings and not via agents.

3. *Future market trends*
- room keys on mobile
- wearable-tech innovation
- innovations in guest acquisition
- property management systems and staff mobility.

4. *Market challenges*
- three other hotels in the area, with similar standards and customer base
- fewer people staying in hotels in recent years.

5. *Their current scenario*
- outdated systems
- an old app with limited functionality
- staff not tech-savvy, need training.

6. *Preconceived ideas*
- They think that my client is just a small start-up and, as such, not stable.

7. *Anxieties in buying from you*
- got something similar
- expensive
- unsure if we're the best on the market
- worry that upgrading the tech each year will be expensive
- think we don't fit in with current tech infrastructure.

8. *Their finite resources*
- budget.

ABI Personal

The buyer in question is the new marketing lead at the hotel and wants to make a big impact quickly, to justify his big salary, and also wants to be at the forefront of an industry he has worked in for a decade.

Pleasure

The technology would make his marketing role far simpler, potentially shortening his working day considerably.

Progress

We positioned the technology to support the buyer's goals: opening more hotels, attracting more guests and, as a consequence, bolstering overall success of the hotel.

Purpose

We ensured he knew precisely how important he was to the entire process, how his creative input and experience was vital and how this would position him as a leader in the innovation of the hospitality sector. We made him fully aware of his role in defining and designing the technology.

RECOGNISING YOUR BUYERS' PSYCHOLOGY

Once we have seen our buyers' reality, we must also get to grips with our buyers' psychology, which means, of course, getting to grips with their mind. This is particularly important in sales, where we need to understand how and why our buyers make the decisions that they do. And unlike our buyers' reality, their decision-making psychology is fixed: it doesn't change and you only need to learn it once.

We have already looked at the large role that intuition plays in our decision-making, and the way that our buyers' decisions are increasingly dictated by gut reactions rather than reasoned thought.

Knowing how to influence the Feeler is therefore a key skill for sellers, and here we will learn how to recognise what is driving our buyers' emotional decisions, and how to use this knowledge in our sales.

Identifying the Emotional Hot Buttons

Far from being rational, our immediate reactions to things are most often triggered by a range of mental shortcuts, or emotional hot buttons – so-called because each relates to a specific feeling or desire. When we appeal to them knowingly, or more often unknowingly, they can be so influential that they are almost guaranteed to generate a reaction.

In every sales scenario, buyers are often desperate to make decisions quickly, with good or bad outcomes for sellers. Understanding which hot buttons to press to interest and excite a buyer, and trigger their emotional decisions, is what good sellers do naturally.

I'm not suggesting that logic plays no role in our decision-making process, but when your buyer is assessing a variety of factors like price and necessity, and calibrating them all, making a decision becomes tiring and difficult.

What is much simpler, in fact almost instantaneous, for your buyer to decide is this:

Do I like them? Have they made it incredibly simple to understand? Are they working with people like me? Do they know my market?

A good seller must therefore become a good psychologist. They must have a solid understanding of how best to use their own mind and a strong intuition in order to identify when to press the right hot buttons.

This knowledge allows us to know what we're looking for in a sales scenario, intuitively: we absolutely don't need to be blind in sales any more. Claude Hopkins, the forward-thinking ad man from Madison Avenue, put it very simply when he said: 'the more [the seller] knows about [psychology] the better. He must learn that certain effects lead to certain reactions, and use that knowledge to increase results and avoid mistakes.' Sellers need to be confident that by pressing a (hot) button there's a strong chance of producing the desired result.

TOOL 8: THE PASSIVE BUYER IMPRESSION

Like a doctor who uses their patients' symptoms to diagnose their illness, a mindful seller has a range of cues or hot buttons they can identify and use to excite their buyers – emotionally.

Unlike the Active Buyer Impression, which needs to be reassessed regularly, the Passive Buyer Impression is something you can learn once. After you have learnt how to recognise the emotional hot buttons, and how to appeal to them, they become part of your knowledge base – in other words, an inbuilt seller toolkit.

The following questions are ones that you can ask yourself to discover what impression you are giving your buyer. Each question relates to a particular hot button that will impact your buyer's decision-making.

The most influential and widest-known hot buttons to be used in selling include: likeability, simplicity, familiarity, authority, urgency, accessibility, quick win, reciprocity, social pressure, and scarcity.

1. Likeability – do they like you?
How likeable you are is hugely important when your buyer is making decisions. This is the basis on which Avon, and more recently the Stella & Dot jewellery business, was founded. At its essence, it means that if we like someone then we're far more likely to buy from them. Buying from our friends, as is the case with Avon and Stella & Dot, is the ultimate in the likeability stakes. We all know we're much more likely to listen and more likely to say yes if it's a friend who is asking for our custom.

As unknown sellers, how can we make sure we're liked? It comes down to the style of our communications, our words and the visuals we choose can be hugely important. We'll examine these choices in detail in Chapter 5, To Think.

On many occasions a seller will move forward too quickly after gaining likeability. They'll jump to the sell – and the sell itself is the antithesis of being likeable. Figuring out how to win over the heart of your buyer must be your first thought and continue throughout the relationship.

2. Simplicity – is your pitch simple?
Simplicity is very important. Not because buyers are stupid, they're just inundated. The simplest story in business will make the most money; the best lawyers know how to simplify complicated stories and win. Simplicity wins out in everything, from business to politics.

In 1979, the Conservatives won the UK election by using a strap line that was just three words: 'Labour isn't working'. And Obama's 2008 campaign was defined by two incredibly simple slogans: 'Hope' and 'Change We Can Believe In'.

Simplicity in sales will get you noticed and understood. The simplest sell will win. There are many routes to simplicity which we'll cover in Chapter 5.

3. Familiarity – are you familiar?
The more often we hear from someone – the more regularly we're
emailed by a firm for example – the more trustworthy they become.
Our attitude towards someone is influenced by the number of times
we're exposed to them.

Of course we have to be careful here: overdo it and you'll be blocked.
Too much will kill the relationship, but there are useful ways and means
to keep in touch without losing face: think about sharing relevant
insights or monthly roundups, for example. This must be considered
carefully, but not ignored; after all, you've got to be 'in it to win it'.

4. Authority – are you an authority?
Do you appear to know what you're talking about? Are you coming
across as an authority in your field? This is a big driver in political
persuasion and one that can be used to powerful effect in our writing
and talking. We like to buy from people who know what they're doing.

An article published in the *New Scientist* in 2015 discussed the idea
that greater success comes to people with louder voices, and research
has revealed that people will judge how confident you are in just 0.2
seconds after first hearing you speak. So confidence in your delivery,
giving the impression of authority is a canny trick.

Authority can also be conveyed in the way you phrase things. So, for
example, rather than saying 'we could help you', switch to 'we will
help you'.

Or rather than 'you could do this', saying 'you should do this'
demonstrates greater confidence in your proposition. This is very
important in selling to crazily crowded markets and we'll explore it in
more detail in Tool 20, The POV.

5. Urgency – are you making it crucial?
Urgency is an underlying influencer and one of the most important
hot buttons impacting our behaviour.

The more pressing you make your offer, the more likely your buyer is to be swayed by your communication.

Does your sell feel urgent? Are you compelling the recipient to respond? Do they need to respond quickly? Will it change the outcome for the better?

6. Accessibility – are you accessible?

Don't make it difficult to buy from you. Changing the status quo requires effort and if it's hard to try or buy, then no one will do it.

Buyers need simple ways to access or understand your product. One way to do this is to break your sell up and let them try one small piece of you.

In a 'try before you buy' scenario, for example, you could make your offer easy to taste, or you could make the inaccessible accessible for a short time period or with limited functionality. We'll examine this in more detail in Tool 48, Taste It.

7. Quick win – can the buyer see a quick win/gain?

Another way to look at breaking your sell up and simplifying it is the idea of marginal gains. Let's not try and make it complicated and solve every problem your buyers have but let's solve something little. Make it very easy and get noticed.

A consumer-focused example: this face cream won't make you look younger but it will give you ten more minutes in bed in the morning. This idea is much more compelling in a sea of products that all profess to make you look younger.

8. Reciprocity – does the buyer owe you something?

We have a deep implanted impulse to repay what someone else gives us. It's what makes us human.

Reciprocity is a powerful force in our social life, as when the neighbour pops round with a bottle of wine at Christmas and you feel compelled to do the same, or when that card arrives from your ancient aunt and you rush to post one in return.

Have you given your buyer something and left a seed in their mind that they now owe you? Examples might include sharing educational content, a testimonial or an invite to an event – even your 'try before you buy' offer.

9. Social pressure – are you already working with people like your buyer?

Without question, when people are uncertain, they use the actions of others to decide how to behave themselves. This hot button is called social pressure or herd mentality. You buy the new brand of yogurt because your friends are eating it; you see on Facebook that a friend has bought something from a brand, or, more compellingly, several friends have, and so you do too. It takes quite a strong character to see others doing something and not want to try the same.

The pull of the group is immensely reassuring and can be a very powerful tool in your selling.

10. Scarcity – are you hard to get?

For something to be desirable, it needs to be hard to get. This is often called scarcity.

We are naturally loss-averse. We hate to lose something or be without something we think we want. One of the cruellest things in love is the fact that the more we can't have someone, the more we want them. Loss aversion is deeply rooted in our psychology.

Not having something, and wanting it, leads you to turn it over and over in your mind, which gives you a thorough knowledge of the product. And yet what we're told to do in sales is the opposite of what makes something desirable. In selling we make something utterly available.

Despite this cue's influence on our decisions, it must be applied with caution as it has been overused in sales. Tricks like 'sign up today or

»PBI«
PASSIVE BUYER IMPRESSION

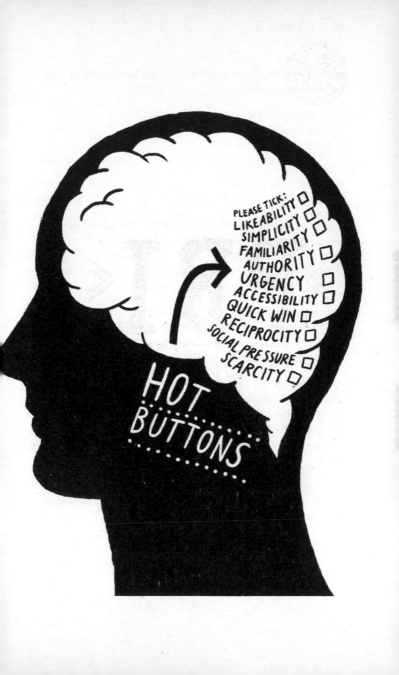

PLEASE TICK:
LIKEABILITY ☐
SIMPLICITY ☐
FAMILIARITY ☐
AUTHORITY ☐
URGENCY ☐
ACCESSIBILITY ☐
QUICK WIN ☐
RECIPROCITY ☐
SOCIAL PRESSURE ☐
SCARCITY ☐

HOT
BUTTONS

you'll miss out' or 'we're running out' won't work. Subtle use will generate the greatest impact.

Examples of using this cue might include:
- I need to check if you qualify.
- Are you good enough?
- It's an incredibly busy time – let's start the project in six weeks.

To demonstrate the usefulness of having these cues at your disposal whilst selling, I'll share this example from my own selling activity.

I was in a situation recently where I had had three meetings with the prospect and gone all the way up through the business to the COO. Everyone loved the concept I had put forward, it solved several internal problems and would enhance pitch wins and ongoing client retention. Rationally, it was a no-brainer for them to say yes.

But two weeks after my final meeting with them I had not received the all-important 'yes please'. A frustrating no man's land for a hungry seller. How could I push them at this stage, acutely aware that the more I push, the more I take the emotional impact away from the scenario?

To win this project I needed to draw upon my knowledge of the social pressure cue. I needed to add urgency and pressure by revealing that we had been asked to build a very similar version of what I was suggesting for someone just like them. So this is what I chose to communicate. Unsurprisingly, I got the 'yes, please' the following week.

I had not changed the offer. It had become no more practically or rationally appealing. I had simply shared information about a similar company wanting the tool, and this provided just the right amount of emotional pressure.

They had been sold, emotionally. The deal was done.

TRY THIS:
The Passive Buyer Impression allows you to keep tabs on what emotional hot buttons you need to recognise and use.

*Look over the elements of the Passive Buyer Impression and ask
yourself the questions. Where could you improve? Could you change
your delivery to appeal emotionally to one or more of these mental
shortcuts? Could you sound more authoritative? Could you increase
your customer contact to make you more familiar? Could you use social
pressure (my favourite)? Success will stem from how well and how
subtly you can enrich your selling with these emotional shortcuts.*

THE RIGHT PRODUCT KNOWLEDGE

To see your buyer is very important, but this isn't quite the full picture.
That requires a full picture of your product, too. Whether selling for an
unknown brand or a global one, achieving a successful and impactful
sale depends on thorough knowledge of what you are selling.

Unfortunately, sellers often fail to understand the importance of
knowing every single detail of their raw material. They are happy
just to accept information about the product from above, taking
seductive shortcuts. Without in-depth product knowledge or client
understanding, they reduce complexity in the wrong places.

If you're selling Google then of course you're in a privileged position,
but you may also have to work harder to position such a well-known
product in order to identify precisely what's relevant in *your* Google
portfolio and overcome any preconceived and negative notions that
your buyers may have. If you're selling an unknown brand or a start-up,
then your challenge is to make your pitch shout 'brilliance'. Trying to do
either of these activities without expert knowledge is hopeless.

TOOL 9: DE-CHUNK

According to cognitive psychologist George Miller, 'chunking' is the
process your brain carries out so you can keep mental control over
lots of information. Your brain essentially packages complex, multi-
faceted ideas into simpler packets, and whatever the volume of

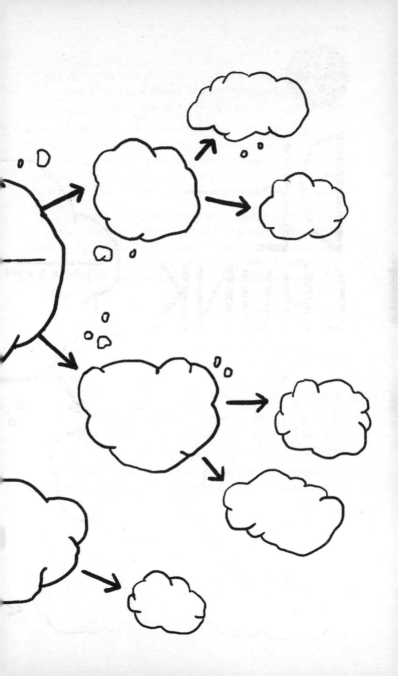

information stored in the chunk, it still only takes up a single space in your working memory. And we have already explored how our working memory's capacity is exceeded very easily.

Chunking is a skill of higher intelligence as it allows us to hold more and learn more, faster – so we readily apply this skill in our life and work. But in a sales scenario, these chunks are a hindrance. When you're trying to gain a clear and detailed picture of your raw material – your product or service – you need the detailed information that lies within the chunks.

Experts on a subject, or sellers who have worked in the same environment for a long time, will have created chunks in their mind – blocks of information about their product usually shrouded in abstraction. For example, you may tend to think of your service as 'data analysis', but what does that actually mean for the buyer? Why are you different from the other thousand firms offering 'data analysis'? What exactly do you do to achieve this?

Or think of your 'client engagement tool'. You can probably break that term down into at least five different features, which are far more valuable for the sales process than the more generic chunk of information will ever be. Open it up into 'regular messaging', 'precise reporting', 'feedback reminders', etc.

I call this process 'de-chunking', as in: opening up what you do and what you're offering, splitting it apart, slicing away the layers, and stripping it back to the core elements.

This is often not so easy to do, since it may have taken years to reach the position of having all your facts neatly chunked. But do it you must.

TRY THIS:
Identify the chunks around your product or service. Can you split these apart and open them up into several different facts about your offer?

De-chunk as far as you can go, until you are left with features a novice in your market would understand. Keep going until you can't de-chunk any more.

TOOL 10: WHAT AND WHY

At the beginning of every new client meeting, in knowledge-collection mode, I start by asking lots of simple questions in an attempt to get all the facts I need in order to sell my client's product.

At this stage it's important not to reduce the knowledge at all. You need it all. If you simplify your product's or offer's features too early, you may miss the most interesting bits – which is catastrophic for your sales impact.

I work with lots of technology firms, helping them create compelling propositions and develop sales campaigns that will generate a successful response. In the kick-off meeting I start by asking *what* and *why* questions. I probe key personnel from these firms to get them to tell me exactly what they offer. They come up with lots of facts but often miss the most crucial information – they miss the meaning. And meaning is crucial, not only to drive behaviour (as we discovered in the ABI personal) but also to ensure what you're selling is understood. Explaining *why* makes your offering crystal clear.

To extract this meaning I prompt them with *why* questions, which helps them to de-chunk their own mental mountain of information. It's important to have completed the ABI before I ask 'why' too, so that my understanding can be related to the buyer as closely as possible. I come to the table with no product knowledge but decades of sales experience, and I don't mind pushing for the answers I need. I keep pushing, in fact, until I have them all, asking for the facts with what can be perceived as an almost childlike urgency. But the facts are crucial, so I keep the questions coming.

In your own sales scenario:

Ask WHAT:
What will give you a clear view of all the facts available, an unbiased view, pre-interpretation. *What* will provide ammunition for the Thinker.

WHAT?

- _____
- _____
- _____
- _____
- _____
- _____
- _____

Why?

-
-
-
-
-
-
-
-

Ask WHY:

Why will help you identify and prioritise the meaning in what you're selling. *Why* will give you content and messaging that will appeal to the Feeler.

TRY THIS:

Think about your product or offer and exactly what it does. De-chunk and break out of industry jargon and explain simply what it is meant to do.

Then explain why. Why does it do the what you've described? Why does it count the clicks or integrate with wider systems? What's the bigger picture here, what is the buyer trying to achieve as their ultimate goal? Why does your offer help with this? And what about personally – does this why tie in with their quest for purpose?

Extract the meaning. The closer you can get to extracting the why and ultimately the purpose of your proposition, the more compelling your sell will be.

TOOL 11: THE EDGE

According to Nassim Nicholas Taleb, statistician, risk analyst and author of the bestselling *The Black Swan*, all the interesting stuff happens at the margin. He calls the territory in which this phenomenon occurs 'Extremistan' (as opposed to 'Mediocristan', where everything is predictably average), and argues that a single outlier observation can have an inordinately large impact.

In line with this argument, it is often as useful, if not more so, to look not at the core of your product for the good stuff but at the facts and details that appear at the margins. Because these could, and probably will, have the biggest impact on your sell.

In the context of your offer or product these will be those features that are outside the core proposition; something in development, or the future potential of your product, or even services that aren't being used by all clients or customers yet. Perhaps think about the most innovative thing about your product, what is unique and most unusual.

Figuring out what these 'outlier' features are and matching them with specific client requirements will have a highly positive effect on your selling.

TRY THIS:
When you're collecting your what and why information, in Tool 10, make sure you include the information at the edges too: the information about your product that might not be immediately obvious or seem that exciting ... yet.

TOOL 12: THREE BUCKETS

The concept of three buckets was first introduced by Adam Morgan in his book *The Pirate Inside*. It works well in helping the technical and the sales people in a company to start working together and thinking about the same questions, and makes selling the product a more collaborative effort. It is also a great way to help you to think about what makes your product great and work out what your customers want to hear.

Collective Intelligence
It's common to have two quite distinct camps of knowledge in an organisation: a bunch of communicators with skills that provoke and persuade but with limited technical knowledge, and a bunch of technical geniuses with thorough technical and industry knowledge. Sellers today must gather the richest, most up-to-date information, and a fast route to it is via these technical experts. Sellers need the stuff that's in these guys' heads.

As sellers, we require a different set of skills from these product experts. They need the skills to make the product great and we need

II

The Edge

CORE

3 BU

the skills to persuade the buyer. These are entirely different but highly complementary business skills.

Gathering and pooling insight from these experts within your business results in what can be described as 'collective intelligence' and is crucial for creating maximum resonance with your target audience.

The biggest issue in gathering this knowledge arises when sales, or indeed any of us, are talking to the person with the technical knowledge. It's a human trait not to feel comfortable asking what we perceive as silly questions. We feel we're giving the impression that we don't 'get it', which can be an uncomfortable place to be. Such reticence is fatal for real success in sales.

The trick here is to make sure we all stop talking past each other when figuring out what actually matters. Embarrassment over silly questions and a lack of knowledge really holds sellers back, and under-explaining is a huge problem between the techies and the communicators. Nobody wants to look bad or ask the stupid question.

I have been doing this for many years and I'm always the one that asks the silly questions. I push until I get it all, down to the very last detail. I know if I don't, my sale won't survive.

TRY THIS:
Get a selection of your product experts in a room – ideally from different parts of the business.

Start with the what and why questions and then ask them to categorise these facts and features into three buckets: what is the same as your competitors, what is better, and what, quite frankly, changes the game?

What's next?
The 'next big thing' is an exciting concept for buyers, who would rather be working with an organisation that will help them into the future than one that's stuck in the past.

Standing still in terms of innovation in your market is seller suicide, particularly in the climate today of rapid, almost monthly transformation in the workplace. It's incredibly important to keep several steps ahead of your buyers. They need to know that by working with you, they will be in a position of strength. You're a faster, more knowledgeable pair of eyes, lighting the darkness ahead.

TRY THIS:
Repeat the Three Buckets exercise, but this time fill in the buckets answering the following questions:
- *What is great about our offer today?*
- *Next year?*
- *And in five years?*

This is a great way to identify and map the future of your product and planned innovations, and to highlight the transformative nature of what you can offer.

Customer intelligence
We identified the customer's reality in Tool 6, the ABI Organisational. This exercise will enable you to gain a clear understanding of what it is about your product that will prove most interesting.

TRY THIS:
For a more customer-centred approach, switch your focus back to the customer and repeat the Three Buckets exercise, this time filling the buckets with your answers to the following questions:
- *What does your product do that your customer can manage without?*
- *What would be useful but not essential?*
- *And what can't they live without?*

Knowing what is crucial will keep your mind focused on what to include in your sales communications.

ink,

'THERE IS INHERENT DRAMA
IN EVERY PRODUCT.
OUR NUMBER ONE JOB IS TO
DIG FOR IT AND CAPITALIZE
ON IT.'
                    LEO BURNETT

This chapter is split into two parts: 'To Think: Synthesising Your Sell' and 'To Think: Communicating Your Sell'.

If you've now had a stab at Tools 1–12, particularly the ABI, then you're in possession of a cauldron-full of raw and accurate knowledge. You have been able to focus long enough to capture information about your buyer and a changing market, and you have stocked your Feeler, drawing on your intuitive psychology to recognise your buyer's decision-making psychology.

This collection of information may be unruly in its current form, but this is precisely what you need in order to move to the next stage of your sell, which requires the second skill of the entire: **to think**.

To think means that you need to interpret and analyse your initial impressions. As the impressionist painter Cézanne noted: 'the eye is not enough ... one needs to think as well'. For sellers, as for Cézanne, seeing is only the first step in the process of uncovering reality. Since reality is actually created by our minds, we must see *and* think in order to communicate this reality to others.

In any sales scenario, **to think** is to spot patterns in the information you've acquired, to pull together the facts that matter and organise them into communications that will strike a chord with your buyer. You now need to distil and interpret your information in order to communicate it for the given sales scenario or recipient. The regurgitation of facts simply won't do here. **To think** is to turn the downright ordinary into anything but. This is what Cézanne did for every simple object he painted.

Extracting the vital element of your offer that will captivate your buyer and lead them to make up their own mind, without outdated or overused techniques, is another underused skill in sales. Identifying the right things to say about your product or story is always dependent on how well you have seen your buyer's circumstances and their psychology; it is directly correlated with how well you have grasped these raw materials.

All of us in sales can learn a great deal from advertising legends David Ogilvy, Leo Burnett and William Bernbach, whose trade – advertising – was to turn the mediocre into the brilliant. They all maintained that the ultimate and most desired skill their employees should have was the ability to think. Burnett highlighted that 'finding the magic things to say about a product that would interest people and lead them by the hand to the conclusion that they should buy something – that was another art, really'. **To think** is a sought-after skill in sales as well as in advertising, and one for which we have the innate mental mechanism, if we just care to use it right.

The essence of thinking effectively is understanding how best to extract, organise and communicate all the facts.

TO THINK: *SYNTHESISING YOUR SELL*

The tools in this first part will enable you to:

- *understand the crucial role of empathy and how to achieve it*

- *extract the information that matters for the buyer in mind*

- *pull together the vast array of facts you have about your product and market and synthesise them in a way that resonates.*

ORGANISE

The challenge here lies in being able to identify the golden nugget in what you're offering. **To think** is an active mental process: we know when we're doing it. It involves our Thinker's basic capacity for pattern recognition, coupled with a drive to combine the disparate, to form separate but related pieces of information into a coherent and compelling story. This act of combination can be described as *synthesis*, and a synthesising mind is the kind of mind we need to adopt.

According to psychologist Howard Gardner, a 'synthesising mind' has the key ability to select crucial information from the copious amounts available, deciding what to pay attention to, what to ignore, and knowing why it makes these choices. Gardner argues this is one of the five essential minds we'll need in the future. Synthesising involves removing the fluff.

Gardner elaborates that 'to synthesise for yourself, you have to put information together in ways which cohere, which make sense for you. And if you are involved in communication, as every teacher, parent, and professional is, the synthesis has to be transmittable to other people.' Being able to communicate the result of your synthesis is another crucial element of being able **to think**.

The desired result of thinking like this is to tell your buyer something which they are open to hearing. You will be able to say something that joins the conversation already in your buyer's mind: they'll understand what you're offering, how it applies to them and will be able to see clearly how they would use it.

It's Not Easy
The information explosion we're experiencing today has only added to the need for effective synthesis. The amount of accumulated information is reportedly doubling every two to three years and sources are vast and disparate. It's in this climate that we seek out coherence; the ability to take information from multiple sources, select the crucial bits, and provide the illumination, is an indispensable skill now and is becoming ever more so each year.

The forces that stand in the way of successful synthesis are many. Trying to master a number of perspectives and then piece them together in a useful way is tricky, to say the least, and engaging yourself in active thought like this is not always easy. The following tool helps you bring the right facts together and remove the surplus facts to ensure the relevant ones have space to sing.

TOOL 13: THE BOW TIE

In most cases, our ability to think actively, to unravel the complex, to spot the patterns and to recombine these into a compelling story, needs a jump start. Our synthesising 'muscle' is often limp and needs developing.

To get to grips with what it takes to carry out a thorough and brutal synthesis, and to extract what it is about your product that will appeal, rationally and emotionally, to your buyer, you can use this tool: The Bow Tie.

TRY THIS:
In the triangle on the left, and using the ABI, write down facts about your buyer's reality. What are their challenges, goals and future trends? The result of your ABI will help you here. Write the key points down in the left-hand side of the bow tie.

The right-hand triangle is all about you. Here you can put the details about your offer, as well as all the information you have collected from Tools 10–12: What and Why, The Edge and Three Buckets.

Now in the space in the middle of the bow tie, identify what it is about your product that directly correlates with something in the buyer's area. Maybe their future trend is a move to the cloud, but they're also anxious about risk. You are on the cusp of launching cloud services and at the edge of your offer is risk capability. Pull this into the main message. This is an effective synthesis. You have identified their requirement and, based on this, have identified something that will excite them and make them prick up their ears. It may not be a central feature of your offering but it is a reality none the less.

e.g.
- *pressure to mov*
to the cloud
- *risk averse*

THEM

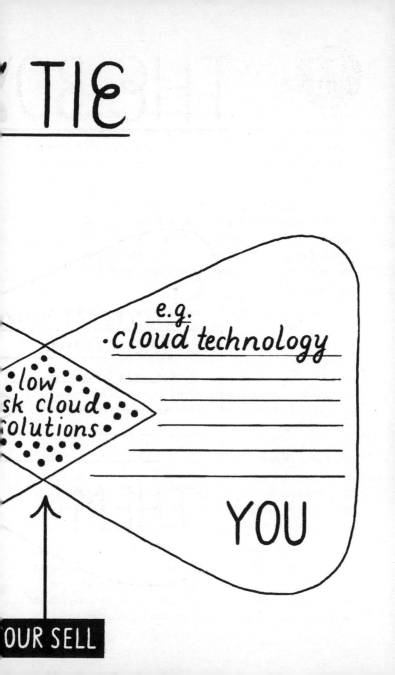

EMPATHISE

As well as the Feeler, we must remember the Thinker in our selling. The Thinker is not only associated with much higher-level thinking and problem-solving, it is also the social part of the brain and the part involved in the skill of understanding others: empathy. And empathy is one of the most crucial skills in sales.

In our mindless state we're increasingly experiencing an inability to genuinely perceive others, and losing our inclination to be empathetic. To really understand other people involves reading their behaviour in terms of their underlying mental states, their desires and intentions; empathy is not easy to achieve when constantly distracted.

Too busy and preoccupied maintaining our own egos, our ability to recognise the psychology of others is diminishing dramatically. In this mental scenario, when we think about how best to position, frame and sell our product, we don't proceed from a place of empathy, with our buyer centrally in mind, but from an egocentric place, with our own worldview as the anchor. This is where we start, and we tend to do no more than adjust from here. This is catastrophic for sales success.

The Role of Empathy

If we really want to understand our buyers, we must put our ego aside and put ourselves in their position. Research, surveys and questionnaires can only tell us so much. In reality, people don't actually know that they want something until they get it.

And so we must imagine for our customers. Sellers need empathy in abundance. How well do you understand your customers? Do you put yourself in their shoes? Imagine what it's like to live in their world, experience their pressures? Do you find this easy or incredibly difficult? Are you too busy, like everyone else, maintaining your own ego?

According to psychotherapist Peter Fonagy, who coined the term 'mentalisation', the key to understanding others is understanding yourself first. Mentalisation is the process 'whereby [through] understanding our own inner experience, we are able to accurately understand others'. In other words, in order to override our mindless approach to how we see our buyers, we must first ensure we know ourselves. What would *we* like to hear? What turns us on – and off – and how would we react to the sales message we're about to share? What would we really think about it? Not the mindless you, but the you with a million-pound budget, huge pressure on performance and a desire to progress your career? Or the you with a tight budget and the desire for an easy life? Would it provoke and persuade you?

If we struggle to understand our buyer's underlying mental states, their attitude towards our product and how we're selling it, then it will most likely be our personal process of mentalisation that is letting us down. We're failing to understand how we genuinely experience the world and, in turn, failing to understand how others see it.

Once we have understood ourselves, then we can move towards true empathy – forgetting our egos completely and putting ourselves in our buyer's shoes. Thomas Messett takes empathy extremely seriously and liked his team at Microsoft to get under the buyer's skin, to 'really get what they're thinking'. Since his team were selling phones, he prompted them to go to a phone store at the weekend: 'I get them to go to a shop, and go through the process. There's nothing better to see things from a customer's perspective.'

Another hard-hitting business-to-business salesman, Bruce Daisley, highlights empathy as the key skill for all members of his vast sales team at Twitter: 'The mindset of the customer is crucial. To have your customer in mind is vital.' David Ogilvy was also adamant in his approach to empathy: 'I never for one minute stopped thinking, "What is my customer thinking?"'

TOOL 14: IN THEIR SHOES

To have any hope of selling you need to know what your buyer needs, wants and desires better than they do: you must become an expert at empathy. The findings from the ABI Organisational and Personal will have helped, but the following simple mental tool will assist you in shifting your thinking from an egocentric standpoint to a more empathetic frame of mind.

TRY THIS:
To help put yourself in the right mindset, take a moment and imagine yourself in the place of your buyer. Start by asking yourself the following questions:

- *If I were the buyer, what sales approach would I like?*
- *What would excite me?*
- *What would I respond to?*

TOOL 15: ETHOS, PATHOS, LOGOS

If thinking and synthesising were simple, then all sales communication would change our behaviour and we'd be persuaded by every sales message we received. After every pitch we'd be left begging for the product – and we all know this simply isn't the case. Far from it.

With that in mind, before we delve deeper into the art of extracting the crucial, it's important to outline what needs to be included in any form of persuasive argument to make sure it's taken seriously.

When the goal is to convince your audience that your product is more valid than someone else's, then you would be advised to draw on the three pillars of persuasion as outlined by the great Greek philosopher Aristotle: ethos, pathos and logos.

Be credible

Ethos means credibility, convincing by the authority of the author. As we discovered in Tool 8, The Passive Buyer Impression, authority is a powerful director of our decisions and we tend to believe people we respect. Unless you're Apple or Google, convincing your buyer that you are credible is about knowledge of your market and how you can bolster your standing in this market. Knowledge will ensure your sell is worthy of respect.

Include emotional appeal

Pathos means persuading by appealing to emotions. Emotional appeal has an enormous influence on decisions and can sway the mind in an instant. To appeal emotionally we must appeal to our buyers' self-interest. And to gain attention we must be mindful of their emotional hot buttons (as covered in the PBI).

Make a clear argument

Logos highlights the role of our rational decision-making. At the heart of all great selling is the argument itself, and this needs to be watertight. We know that emotion has a strong influence on our decisions, and emotional appeal might save your sales email from immediate deletion. But emotion alone is not enough. Your central argument must be clear in order for your sell to resonate with your buyer, and thus be clearly persuasive. Emotion with no rational reason means you're unlikely to prevail. Your central argument, which you will have begun to create in your bow tie, can be expressed directly or indirectly, but the strength of your claims will impact your sell.

By thinking about all three crucial prongs – ethos, pathos and logos – you will ensure that you develop a very compelling communication.

TRY THIS:

Use these pillars as a means to develop your sell. Before you construct your sell, ask yourself these questions:

IN THE

IF I WERE THE BUYER
WHAT SALES APPROACH
WOULD I LIKE?
WHAT WOULD EXCITE ME?
WHAT WOULD I
RESPOND TO?

←

R SHOES

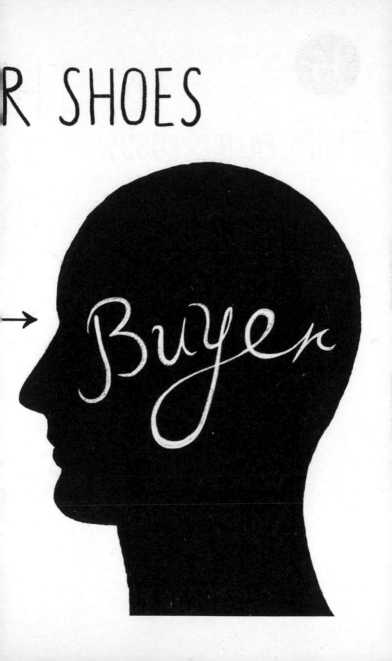

ETHOS, PATHOS, LOGOS

Ethos

Logos

YOUR SELL

- *How do I ensure I sound like I know what I'm talking about?*
- *How do I extract the emotional elements from my sell to ensure that these are crystal clear?*
- *How can I use the hot buttons?*
- *What is my watertight argument as to why they should buy my product? How do I make this clear in a way that will immediately resonate?*

Use this knowledge of the foundations of a good argument as you work through the next tools – you should ensure that you regularly appeal to ethos, pathos and logos.

SIMPLIFY

As early as 1900, philosopher Henri Bergson was very aware of the demands of everyday living on our attention, and our need to wear blinkers in order to filter the flow of information heading our way. He wrote extensively about the woeful inefficiency of our sight, and how, to deal with the vast array of interruptions, we only want to receive what is immediately relevant and consider what is immediately practical. Our buyers don't have the time or mental energy to analyse all the information that comes their way; instead, as Bergson suggests, they only see what is relevant and practical. And these are two central attributes that will determine if your sell is taken seriously, or not.

In the *Psychological Bulletin* in 1992, Nalini Ambady and Robert Rosenthal discussed 'thin-slicing', which can be defined as 'our unconscious tendency to make snap judgements based on only narrow windows of experience'. This is a great way to think of what your buyers are going to do when they receive your sales communication. They're defaulting decisions to their Feeler, resorting to snap judgements. And these quick decisions, based on minimal information, will most often remain unchanged.

It's crucial, then, if you want to get noticed, to interpret your raw materials in just the right way. For buyers to even notice what you do, you will need to adopt a brutal simplicity of thought and develop a strong preference to get to the point. Your mind must be attuned to sort the wheat from the chaff. To synthesise.

William Bernbach, who founded the global advertising agency DDB in 1949, encouraged all his employees to simplify at all costs: 'You must be as simple and as swift and as penetrating as possible. And it must stem from knowledge. And you must relate that knowledge to the consumer's needs.' Bernbach underpinned all his work with insight into human nature, respect for the consumer and the power of creativity; even today this is the guiding mantra at the agency, now 4,000 people strong.

Unearthing this practical simplification of reality is a key step in your synthesis for any given customer. Bobette Buster, storytelling consultant for Disney, calls this gem of information the 'gleaming detail ... a singular, elegant moment of clarity'. For each customer there is a gleaming detail about your offer that is the most compelling and will immediately interest them. Highlighting that gleaming detail is very similar to the aim of an 'elevator pitch' – the idea that you can define your proposition so that the summary can be delivered in the time span of an elevator ride. And whilst the content of this type of pitch may have evolved, with a far greater emphasis on the recipient, the idea of extracting the essential facts remains true.

This vital information, the gemstone in a pit of rock, is the 1 per cent of your offer that will give life to the other 99 per cent. It's the individual element that will enhance the rest and it's the killer fact that, to your prospect, will differentiate you specifically from your competitors. This is the anchor you need at the centre of your story and should be the compass point you return to in all your ongoing communication with your buyer. Simplicity here is crucial and identifying this bit of your sell is called your 'hook'.

TOOL 16: THE HOOK

To achieve your hook, you need to use the information you have acquired in Tools 5–15 – your buyer's business goals, challenges, emotional drivers and anxieties, and the full gamut of information about your product – and select what it is about your product that is immediately relevant and practical for your prospective buyer. Having de-chunked your product into more accessible themes and terms, you can now rebuild these chunks into something that is compelling, with the buyer centrally in mind. The complete knowledge you have acquired will prevent you from leading with the wrong bits.

As I highlighted when discussing the ABI, it's crucial here that you look beyond solving your buyer's immediate challenges. This is commonly known as the 'solution' or 'value' sell: you position your product as the solution to the buyer pain you have identified. But this kind of sales pitch is no longer enough, and your hook must demonstrate a greater understanding of your buyer, beyond their challenges.

Why? Because the value sell has always been about solving problems, and communicating what value you add as a solution. But if your value is 'increased sales', then how does this differ from the hundred other services which all promise the same thing? Communicating the value in your product is of course relevant, but you can no longer rely on this information alone. In this climate, your hook must differentiate you from the rest.

The right hook should be used in prospecting, pitches and conversation, to reiterate your relevance. Working out the hook is a seller must-do and your hook is as transient as your buyer's reality. It will vary depending upon recipient, stage in the sell and communication medium.

With this in mind, you will most likely need several hooks in the course of your sell. One for prospecting and the early stages, which will be concerned with your buyer's direct departmental challenges. And one for the later stages, as the sale moves along, when your hook must encompass knowledge of the buyer's bigger organisational goals. At any given stage in a sale, the hook is the story you need to tell to guarantee maximum resonance with your intended recipient, across that particular communication channel.

Put simply, the hook is about telling your buyer what you have to offer so that it is utterly relevant for them at that very moment. And framing it in terms they'll care about.

Hookless

A friend of mine is responsible for several million pounds-worth of new business annually for a media firm. In a bid to generate interest for a new initiative, her boss had reached out via email to twenty CEOs. He composed and sent out a message saying, 'Hello, I like what your brand is doing, we're doing this, let's talk,' relying on his name and reputation (ethos alone) to generate a clamour of keen responses. None came.

Why such a poor return? His message was clear and it was simple. But fatally, it didn't contain the hook. He'd given the recipients nothing to get excited about. What he needed to do was to work out the gleaming detail about his proposition for each recipient, what precisely this audience needed to hear. And add an emotional punch.

The results from the ABI and Tool 5, Four Things, would have revealed the collective challenges shared by this audience, what they all need to do more, better or faster, plus their personal goals. And Tool 9, De-chunk, would have broken out his key product variables. Knowing all this would have provided the information needed to create the perfect hook.

And a really relevant hook would have changed his response rate quite dramatically.

16

The Hook

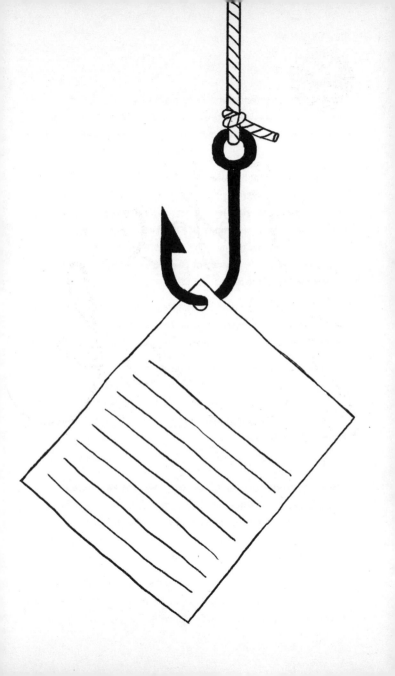

Example 1

Working with an international PR firm offering a whole host of communication services to the market, we needed to extract the hook for their buyers: heads of marketing and heads of PR in large blue-chip firms.

The ABI revealed that our client's central goal was increasing direct sales. This was the linchpin but not necessarily the hook. The secondary goals included upping media coverage, recognising the need for heightened impact in a market experiencing high competition for share of voice. This was coupled with another secondary need for measurement of any creative endeavour. All these together made up the hook.

The PR agency's *what* was the technology at the centre of all of their work, which had the unique capability of being able to scan the online media landscape and uncover any gaps relevant for their buyer.

The *why* was that this unique information enabled their client's content and messages to plug these gaps in the media, which in turn maximised press coverage and informed creative direction. The unique tool also measured changes in volume of coverage, allowing for accurate reporting.

This is one of the hooks we used:

'The unique software enables you to uncover the gaps in your relevant media landscape, which informs laser targeting of content and longer-term creative direction. Importantly, the tech enables real-time data on improved performance. And we're running the software for several retail firms including ... and ...'

We hit their goals head on (the *what* and *why* were very clear) and added an emotional punch by using social pressure and mentioning a couple of similar firms we're working with.

Example 2

We worked with a leadership-development firm running a range of leadership programmes, whose buyers were heads of Learning and Development in large professional services firms. It became clear following the ABI that the buyers' secondary goal was to equip leaders within their businesses with the skills to cope with rapid technological developments, particularly in this climate of change and uncertainty. Certainty would bring them peace of mind and provide them with the confidence to create future-focused strategies. The central goal of the buyers was increasing market share, but this wasn't a message we would use in this communication (we'll look in detail at the difference between big and small messaging in Tool 19, Think Big and Small).

The buyers' preconceived idea was that the majority of development programmes are time-consuming and inaccessible to their global, time-short and transient leadership workforce.

A simple hook we needed to communicate was:

'The programmes prepare leaders for the next ten years and for rapid and diverse transformations in technology, employee demands and buyer habits. For large professional services firms, we run online, on-demand modules accessible for your busy leaders.'

Again, we addressed their fears head on (the *what* and *why* were very clear) and added the emotional impact by mentioning 'large professional services firms' making the hook feel utterly relevant and suitable.

Example 3

A financial technology client selling to investment firms wanted to appeal to a new breed of boutique mini-brokers. The ABI revealed that these smaller brokers' central goal was to compete on the same level as larger brokers. A secondary goal included wanting to keep up to speed with changes in regulation. And their preconceived idea was that this software was an expensive tool. Their finite resource was a limited budget for such software.

A hook was simple:

'The tool enables mini-primes to upscale manual procedures, navigate regulation and position themselves to compete with larger primes. The tech is available on a per-module basis, enabling you to tailor the set-up according to precise commercial objectives.'

We homed in on their precise requirements and made sure we addressed the cost barrier by highlighting the 'per module' set-up.

TRY THIS:
Look at your findings from Tools 5–15 and, with your buyer in mind, develop your hook. The key here is not thinking about what they 'should' care about, but adopting an empathetic frame of mind and communicating what they really 'would' care about. Tell them the facts, include why, and make sure their emotional drive is taken into account.

Think about all the information you have collected in Chapter 4, To See, and the synthesis you came up with in Tool 13, The Bow Tie, and create your hook from the most relevant connections.

The following three tools are about playing with and bolstering your hook. This is only possible with a complete picture of your buyer.

TOOL 17: THE STRETCH

Identifying your hook and framing your product so that it resonates might be incredibly easy; more likely is that it's not easy at all. Sometimes what is relevant is inherent and at the heart of your product, and what you're offering is suitably practical and enticing. Sometimes it isn't immediately obvious and you need to 'stretch' to the edges of your proposition to ensure that you excite.

The stretch is a device to shift the hook to being about a more specific product feature on the periphery that makes more sense for the buyer.

This is a handy tool in very competitive markets with lots of product choice.

Example

Working with a leading newspaper, we needed to make their job site relevant and enticing to a new target clientele: niche recruitment firms. The ABI revealed that these firms had small budgets, and that their preconceived idea was that this newspaper's job site was expensive and crowded and, as such, not suitable for their purposes.

We were acutely aware of their need to redefine their commercial packages, so we looked at the edge of our client's product and at the information available from the Three Buckets – both collective intelligence and the future of the product. At the edge of their proposition was the story of fixed-priced advertising packages with analytics built into the price. This wasn't their central sell – far from it – but it was this detail that was most likely to excite this smaller buyer audience.

By offering a fixed-price package, we had taken away the risk of spiralling costs, and with built-in measurement, the advert could be assessed for success immediately.

We had been able to stretch and summarise the offer as follows:

'This fixed-price, direct-response package allows niche agencies access to our relevant and unrivalled candidate base. In other words, you can understand what's working, when and exactly how much it has cost you.'

17

The
Stretch

YOUR OFFER »———————•
_____
_____
_____
_____
_____
_____
_____

→ THE STRETCH

We stretched the proposition to ensure resonance. And it worked.

Notice how the stretch here included detail about the buyer's preconceived idea (the expense of the adverts) as well as their goals and challenges.

TRY THIS:
Use the Edge tool here and the results from the Three Buckets tools. Do any of the facts here resonate more readily with your understanding of the buyer's reality – the information you discovered in the ABI? Now make these the centre of your sell, make this your hook.

TOOL 18: THE MAGNIFY

The Magnify is an alternative tool to ensure you're able to highlight your most relevant features and deliver an empathetic sell.

Look at your findings again from Tools 5–15 and think about what it is about your offer that is most enticing for your buyer. Which bit of your offer or which particular feature is the hook, the bit that will immediately resonate and excite?

If it's on the edge, this feature may not sound hugely exciting; it may not be the star performer. The job of the Magnify is to exaggerate its importance and make that the central story.

Example
Working with a provider of outdoor fitness classes, we used the ABI to reveal that the major challenge of their target buyers (mums) was trying to squeeze their fitness schedule into their extremely busy life of juggling family and job.

Our client's sell was focusing on the benefits of the classes, the bolstered health advantages and the low cost of bulk-buying sessions. Interesting stuff, but not enough to differentiate this product from others, or resonate fully with the target market.

We identified that drop-in sessions – something our client already offered – would provide an effective hook. It was on the edge of their proposition, and they weren't shouting about it. So we developed a campaign which magnified the range of drop-in times available.

Like this:

'We run tailored drop-in sessions, four times a day, for ambitious, health-conscious and time-stretched mums, enabling the impossible: a consistent exercise regime for noticeable results.'

This offer was on the edge of the firm's core service but we magnified its central importance for maximum resonance with a particular audience.

TRY THIS:
Look at everything about your product, right to the edge; be sure to relate this to your buyers' goals and challenges.

If the relevant hook is not your central feature, magnify its importance. Exaggerate it – empathetically.

Don't Forget!
It's important to flag here that there is a big difference between the Stretch and the Magnify – and trickery. Highlighting and exaggerating the features of your product so they meet the buyers' needs is very different to making things up and creating features that don't exist. That will never work in a sales environment and any sign of trickery will result in resentment from the buyers' side. These tools are about making what's already there more visible and appealing. They are about enhancing empathy.

The

Magnify

TOOL 19: THINK BIG AND SMALL

When receiving your sales communication, your buyer needs to know how you can take them from A, their current situation without you, to B, which in most cases is their big-picture goal, whether that is sales, increased followers, greater return on investment, or effectively trained employees.

To resonate and make an impact, you must describe your offer to deliver B directly, or clearly communicate how you deliver a crucial step towards this. The idea of incremental gains is another way to look at this: making your product the means to the end, and not simply the end.

Your offer may take the buyer directly to B or, more likely, may be a step in this journey. Both can be equally powerful propositions, but you must be able to see both scenarios and position yourself to offer the most relevant. And make it clear which one you are offering.

If in reality you have no chance of getting your buyer directly to B, then don't even attempt to offer it – you will fail every time.

Example 1
We worked with a provider of data analytics whose target clients were TV channels desperate for data on their viewers. The ABI revealed that the buyer's central goal, their 'B', was increasing advertising revenue. This was their big picture and the ongoing challenge for the majority of media companies.

To position our client's product as solving this challenge directly would have been a step too far for the sell to work. We'd be competing with the buyer's advertising sales team and a whole host of other service providers. This is not where we needed to be in order to guarantee the interest we required.

The buyer's secondary goal, and the steps that led towards B, the big picture, was their desire to acquire and retain more viewers, both huge contributors to the end goal.

This is where we needed to focus our sell and so we positioned ourselves here, with the bigger picture close at hand as our linchpin.

We summed up the sell like this:

'Through the unique, real-time data we collect, you will understand your digital audience on a granular level and, in turn, can actively enhance their viewing experience.'

Of course this in turn will help them acquire and retain more viewers, and provide the crucial ammunition needed to grow all-important advertising revenue. But to have sold at this level would not have differentiated our client.

Example 2

Working with a financial software firm selling to wealth-management firms, we found that their buyer's central goal was maximising investor return, but that they had lots of secondary challenges, including trying to juggle many different day-to-day administrative and compliance-related tasks.

The sell went like this:

'Our technology allows you to maintain regular communication with all your stakeholders, producing accessible and visually compelling reports with little manual effort.'

Of course this will enable them to maintain their focus on maximising return for investors, but we didn't need to spell it out. If we had, we would have joined a host of services all offering the same benefit.

TRY THIS:
Think about how you solve your buyer's big challenges and/or support their quest to reach their central goal.

Use this knowledge to communicate your product either as the direct means to their end or, more likely, as a key step on the journey.

THINK BIG

TOOL 20: THE POV

Being able to synthesise your raw materials into a coherent argument and create a hook will always be an essential skill. But in many sales scenarios, particularly in competitive markets, you may need something extra. You need to tailor your pitch so that you not only resonate, but you also teach something new and provoke a reaction from your buyer. For this you will need to develop a clear point of view (POV).

In 2013, the Corporate Executive Board (CEB) surveyed over 6,000 sales reps and identified five types of seller: the Hard Worker, the Challenger, the Relationship Builder, the Lone Wolf and the Reactive Problem Solver. Each type has skills that make them good sellers, but the one that consistently outperforms all the others is the Challenger. Not only do Challengers *tailor* their sell to their buyer's needs for maximum resonance, but they also *teach* their buyers about new ideas, offering fresh perspectives on their business, and, finally, they aren't afraid to be assertive, to stand up to the buyer and *take control* of the sale.

By learning to highlight relevance and create a hook with Tools 16–19, you now know how to tailor your sale so that it resonates with your buyer. But having a point of view and communicating this with authority could be the final differentiator you need, which will allow you to both 'teach' and 'take control' in your sale.

In practice, the Challenger applies these skills by providing customers with surprising and creative insights into how they can compete in their current market, save or make money, or revolutionise current practices (we'll examine creative thinking in Chapter 6, To Improve). Challengers don't just rely on relevance; they bolster their sale by provoking the buyer.

The Challenger Sale by Matthew Dixon and Brent Adamson from the CEB elaborates this idea: 'The battle for customer loyalty is won or lost long before a thing ever gets sold. And the best sales reps win that battle not by "discovering" what customers already know they need, but by teaching them a new way of thinking altogether.'

To achieve this, you must be in the possession of a unique understanding of the world that you can impart to your buyer. You need to be able to tell them something new. Your POV should stem from a complete picture of your buyer (the tools in Chapter 4, To See, will have helped with this) but not end here – you need to offer a perspective on the situation that is all your own, and be determined in your delivery of it.

Identifying your POV

In order to identify your POV, you must first examine your buyer's reality. *What* have you spotted in your buyer's world that suggests 'this is broken!', or in their wider market that shouts 'the world is moving here!'? Use Tools 11 and 12, The Edge and Three Buckets, to help you.

Now think about *why* the thing you've spotted is such a big opportunity. Why would it make sense for you to pursue this avenue rather than another? Thinking about why you are focusing on something will give your POV its strength.

Recently, in my own selling, I was reminded of how effective a strong POV can be. Examining the activity of a media sales team, it was clear that whilst this well-known brand could use its name to generate meetings with potential buyers, closure rate was extremely poor. On average, only one in ten meetings resulted in any business.

Why? In my opinion, it was because the sales team weren't asking deep enough questions, and this was resulting in responses that weren't based on the right insight.

I had my *what* and *why* and could generate my POV. With this point of view I was able to explain not just that the sellers needed to be better at closing deals, but what they needed to change in order to be so.

This POV resulted in my suggestion of a digital platform that would enable the sellers to share a predetermined set of empathetic questions with their buyers. This removed the need for a long and laborious discovery phase, and ensured that sellers asked deep questions that resulted in relevant insights. The sellers could in turn

20 THE POV

YOU

»

»

What's the problem/opportunity ?

Why is it important ? (5x)

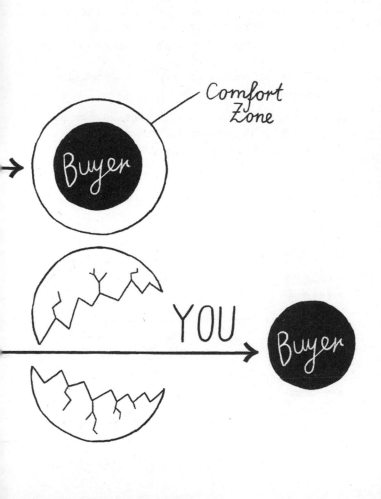

be confident their proposal matched precise commercial objectives, and the buyers could be certain that the seller accurately understood their needs.

Communicating your POV

This was a novel idea, new to this particular market. I was challenging the status quo and taking my buyer out of their comfort zone. Authority in my delivery and a consistent message was crucial. My clear argument, based on a knowledgeable point of view, enabled the project to get the go-ahead, and the tool has now enhanced closure rate considerably.

With an unusual and persuasive point of view, based on complete knowledge of your buyer's market, you can take control of the conversation and lead the buyer where you want.

TRY THIS:

To formulate your POV, think hard about your buyer's situation and the future of their market.

What have you spotted that could be the big opportunity that they're not yet capitalising on? What is broken that they haven't spotted yet?

Why does this offer such a powerful opportunity? Why is it so crucial that it's fixed?

Once you have the answers to these questions, ask yourself 'why' again: why is it important? Why should they care? Keep asking 'why' until you have a clear argument.

Make sure your POV is a position you can defend. Remember that you want to challenge your buyer's current activity, and not just fit in with it. You want to break your buyer out of their comfort zone. A strong POV will allow you to challenge your buyer's ideas and provoke them into seeing things your way. Be assertive, but don't bully.

Once you have your POV, you can use Tools 21–34 to communicate it.

TO THINK: *COMMUNICATING YOUR SELL*

The tools in this section will help you:

- *say the right things and use the right language to ensure you get read first and sell more*

- *rethink the ways you communicate, from email to WhatsApp and face-to-face, using techniques to structure and frame your sell*

- *grasp the possibilities of non-verbal communication, through using compelling methods such as visuals to resonate emotionally with your audience.*

It's noisy out there, so the way you share your sell is as important as what you're offering. *How* you say and communicate your sell carries as much weight as *what* you say.

Tools 16–20 have ensured you'll get noticed by recognising and extracting the individual and differentiating elements about your offer.

We now turn to Tools 21–34, which focus on how to frame your pitch in order to effectively communicate this relevance: how to pick which words to use, how to structure your pitch and how to create pictures in your buyer's mind. And, most importantly, how to appeal emotionally, how to excite the Feeler and generate the all-important response: 'I want that.' This is crucial.

Information overload means that buyers tend to pay closer attention to the people who are explaining than to the explanation itself.

With buyer decisions increasingly stemming from the Feeler, the way you share your sell will evoke the emotional response in your buyer. They'll love what you have to say or they'll hate it – and they'll decide very quickly. To appeal emotionally, we must pay attention to our buyers' hot buttons, outlined in the PBI, and learn to explain ourselves so that we resonate emotionally.

Your Language

According to Steven Pinker, language – a uniquely human skill – is a biological instinct and responsible for the rapid advances in human evolution, due to our ability to use it to learn from each other. Having language allowed us to tell stories, and using stories we were able to relay our experiences to the next generation; in this way, each generation progressed faster and further than the previous one.

Our ability to use language is arguably the greatest invention of human civilisation, as well as being an innate skill. We're able to convince others just with our words and equally we're able to repel, to lose and to hurt.

A Mental Picture

The language we create, whether relaying details of our holiday to a friend or describing our product to a buyer, enters the listener's mind, where their mental processes transform the language into an image for them to compute. With as much of a third of our brain's functionality dedicated to sight, we don't actually think in language but in pictures. This is what enables us to make decisions quickly.

Imagine that I told you I'd bought a house in the country last year. Are you thinking of the letters **H O U S E** or do you have an image of a country cottage in your mind?

In order for buyers to understand what we're selling, our language must allow them to create the right picture. How we use language and how we use pictures are essential steps in effective communication.

The following tools focus on the order of the words, and the individual words themselves, to ensure the language you use forms the right image in your buyer's mind, and in turn makes your sell suitably persuasive.

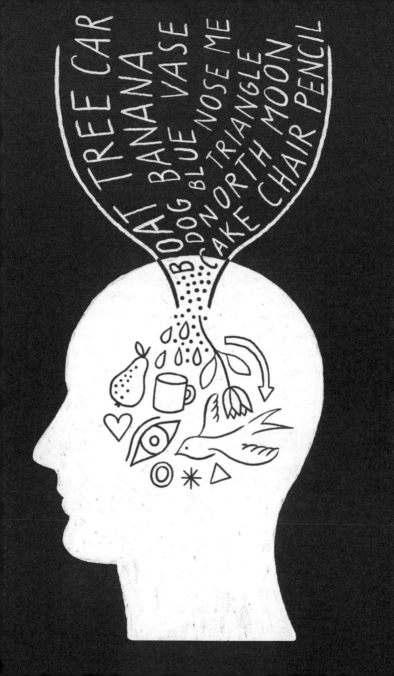

WORDS: IN THE RIGHT ORDER

Storytelling is a powerful form of communication and it is through stories that we learn about one another. A good story, told well, will resonate emotionally and will always leave the listener feeling something.

In a sales context, facts by themselves are not a very effective means of communication; they are too hard to compute, and can often involve an overwhelming number of statistics or plain statements that leave the listener cold. Stories are much more engaging; when we're trying to decide if something is right for us or not, stories allow us to picture ourselves in the scenario and imagine what it would be like if we used that product. Logic likes to generalise, whilst stories capture the specific information and emotion, enabling our buyers to grasp what we do and figure out if they like it, almost instantly.

When we use stories in our sales communication, our buyers are far more likely to be able to form visual images which will help them remember the pitch. Stories involve structure, use concrete images, realistic details and devices such as metaphor and antithesis – all the building blocks for creating a great pitch, too.

TOOL 21: THE STORY STAR

Rudyard Kipling, author of the most famous simple tales, the *Just So Stories*, gave an insight into his extraordinary storytelling talent in this little rhyme:

> I keep six honest serving men
> (They taught me all I knew);
> Their names are What and Why and When
> And How and Where and Who.

The key pins of any great story are *what, why, when, how, where* and *who*. If you think about your product and can answer all these questions (*what* and *why* should be easy if you've already done Tool 10), then this is a fantastic start when framing your sell.

These are the central coordinates for telling your sales story, and are what people need to know to be able to grasp what you're telling them. In all scenarios, try to answer these and you will make your sell very clear.

Example
A client of ours, a city-based fitness firm, was sharing their story like this: 'By choosing ABC Corporate Pilates you have the guarantee that we're able to deliver the fitness results your employees need to achieve the business results that you demand.' This is generalised, overly factual, highly ignorable communication.

We employed Kipling's advice and reworked their story like this:
- what: updated Pilates
- why: because you need some supportive supervision – otherwise you might cheat
- when: in your lunch hour
- how: using machines
- where: Hoxton
- who: the time-short, ambitious professional.

'Based in Hoxton, offering lunchtime classes, we're Pilates updated for today's time-short, ambitious professional. With machines that target specific muscle groups, you essentially have your own personal trainer for fifty minutes – so no cheating.'

The complete story is told empathetically in two short sentences, and enables the recipient to imagine themselves in the scenario mentioned.

TRY THIS:
Answer as many of these six story prompts as you can: write down the who, what, where, when, why and how of your product. You can imagine them arranged like a star, as in the visual for this tool, with the customer at the centre. Now take those elements and put them together in a concise way, arranging them into a sell that will make your proposition crystal clear in the mind of your buyer.

The Story Star

WHERE ....

WHEN ....

W ....

BUTER

W ....

WHAT

HOW

TOOL 22: THE REALITY CHECK

In order to make a story emotionally powerful, it must mirror in some way the reality of its audience: the more specific the moment of recognition, the better.

The same is true in the very best selling. The closer you get to the buyer's reality, with a statement that will immediately ring true, the more they will understand you and take you seriously. The best storytelling, and the best selling, hones in on a moment in time. This again allows a mental picture to build in the audience's mind.

Homing in on a real-life moment, bringing flat language to life by enabling the buyer to picture themselves in the scenario, is an incredibly useful tool when selling. Disney's Bobette Buster says, 'You need to find that one image that connects with the audience, that aha moment.'

Focusing on the moment is a great time to use the hot button of social pressure: to tell your buyer about something you have done recently for someone just like them. And, in turn, to incorporate a further persuasive emotional punch into your sell.

Example:
- 'Over the past three months we've been working with Babel to ensure that their leadership is acutely aware of how the retail industry is changing and which disruptive forces they should prioritise.'
- 'Our recent work with Linear, a UK-based mini-prime, has allowed them to upscale fast by enabling the shift from clunky manual reconciliation to the automation of this crucial activity.'
- 'In the autumn, the association of hairdressers used our data to understand the styling habits of their 14,000 members.'

TRY THIS:

Think about a moment in time that could relate to your buyer. Have you recently completed a great project or had a great success? Can you home in on a specific feature of your product and how it worked in reality?

Now write this description down, imagining you are telling a potential new client about the event.

TOOL 23: WHAT YOU'RE NOT

Describing what you're *not* can make it really clear what you actually *are*. This is particularly true in a crowded marketplace, where such an exercise will differentiate you from your competitors. This is a useful way to describe yourself, to make yourself understood and remove any ambiguity. It enables you to spell out what you *do* do, by making it absolutely clear what you don't do.

Think about this in your personal life and notice how vocal people are in their distaste for things: 'I am not a Morrissey fan,' for example. By describing what we are not, we feel that we're making our identity perfectly clear.

Example

Working with a software client in the mega-crowded social-media tools market, we used this method to explain why we differed.

'We're not a social-measurement tool. We analyse language on an industrial scale – we don't simply measure the volume of conversations, but examine precisely how your customers talk'.

TRY THIS:

Is there a grey area in your product specification? Is it clear for buyers to see your differentiation in the market?

Is there something that you feel the rest of the market is getting wrong?

To set yourself apart, and to make it crystal clear, try describing not what you are, but what you are not.

22

LIFE

*The
Reality
Check*

Ø

WHAT YO

RE NOT

TOOL 24: THREE STEPS

The foundation of any great story has three steps: a beginning, a middle and an end. In fiction this is called the dramatic framework.

We are very familiar with this framework; our minds are attuned to this pattern of progress and understand it quickly. In a three-step sell, the beginning sets the scene and introduces the variables, the middle is the meat in the story – what actually goes on to make change happen – and the end is the improved scenario. Just as any basic mechanical process has an input, a process and an output.

When you have all the knowledge of your sell and can see it clearly, you will notice that your sell will fall naturally into three stages. This is partly due to the ability of your working memory to hold this volume of information, and partly due to our minds being at ease with this three-step framework.

Example 1

For a financial-technology client, we created this 3-step story:

'Our technology is valuable for ambitious prime brokers keen to capitalise on recent market developments. We enable you to consolidate all your vital data, offer complete lending protection and the result ensures your operations are comparative with larger primes.'

Another three-step framework which also appeals to our desire for simplicity is dividing the sell into just three words. This is called the 'rule of three' and is an eye-catching and persuasive way to display information.

The French knew this well and rallied the entire nation with: '*Liberté, égalité, fraternité*' (liberty, equality, fraternity). As did Mars with their slogan: 'A Mars a day helps you work, rest and play.'

Example 2
For the financial-tech client this rule of three worked rather well. In three words, the technology enables the buyer to 'consolidate, protect and grow'.

TRY THIS:
Let your sell fall naturally into three distinct stages – the input, process and output, or three specific steps towards improvement.

Tell your sales story like this, in three simple stages.

And then simplify into three words.

THE WORDS THEMSELVES

Do buyers really notice how something is actually written today? Absolutely.

Your buyers are wading through opaque prose day in, day out. If you want to appeal to their quick reactions and the Feeler, then you need to know how to use words effectively. Getting understood means taking the individual words you use very seriously.

Good grammar is certainly important, but for our purposes I'm going to discuss what words and style of language will create the greatest excitement, make the biggest impact and help you sell more.

David Allen, author of *Getting Stuff Done*, is a big fan of minor improvements leading to massive change: 'When you know what you're doing, efficiency and style are your only improvement opportunities'. When you know what you're selling, and have figured out your hook, then style will be one of your only means of improving your pitch.

There is a fine line between what a good seller puts into their sales communication and what an unsuccessful seller leaves out. When writing there are certain key attributes that will determine

1

INPUT

2

PROCESS

3

OUTPUT

whether you are taken seriously or ignored. I have studied reams of sales writing, thousands of sales emails and pitch documents, and even had my sales language analysed by clever language software. Through this exercise, key characteristics of successful selling clearly emerged: a human approach, free from cliché, use of simple language, with added energy and urgency and an authoritative style.

The most important thing is that your words aren't ignored. Writing to sell is not about winning prizes for writing, but about selling more. David Ogilvy's famous line goes: 'The way to sell is to get read first.'

CUT THE CLICHÉ

Wanting to sound like other people is incredibly tempting but has limited impact in any sales scenario. The more original you can be, the more interesting you will become, and the more you will stand out – and that's the goal.

Over-used and well-known sales clichés make the sales effort more obvious and is likely to provoke corresponding buyer resistance. Uniqueness is what will mark the best sellers apart from the rest.

Good writing is not necessarily a natural gift. You have to learn to write well. Our natural instinct is to talk, to blurt it all out. But as the written word is the medium of choice for our buyers, we must all learn to write well to get ourselves read and understood.

Tools 25, 26 and 27 will help bring your words to life.

TOOL 25: GET PHYSICAL

With our knowledge of our product concealed in chunks, we can tend to use opaque terms when writing to sell, such as 'efficiencies', 'productivity' or 'deliverables'— which could each mean different things to different buyers.

To break out of this you must shift your mindset and use more concrete language: words and terms that immediately make sense and are clear to anyone who may not have expert knowledge. This includes physical details about the product or offer, details that are often left out of communications.

The chunked examples below have left out the real nature of the product; the writer is presuming the reader will already know this, or will care enough to de-chunk the pitch for themselves. This chunked language takes many things for granted.

Here is an example of a chunked sentence:

'We provide a platform that enables you to increase efficiencies and reduce operational costs while fully engaging with your guests.'

With lots of knowledge of your product and market, you may be bored of explaining it simply, but the buyer needs to hear it that way. The use of concrete language, on the other hand, prevents any confusion:

'We've paid close attention to what your guests want in a hotel app, enabling you to keep them happy – before, during and after their stay.'

TRY THIS:
Carry out a de-chunk of your product or service using Tool 9. Using the revealed details, attempt to explain what you're offering using physical, concrete language.

Use the visual for Tool 25 to write down your chunked language on the left side, and how you might explain it in far simpler language, on the right.

GET F

PRODUCT FEATURE

e.g.   Twitter Monitoring

》

HYSICAL

CONCRETE LANGUAGE

e.g. we collect and count clicks

TOOL 26: THE METAPHOR

A metaphor is a figure of speech in which a word or phrase that ordinarily designates one thing is used to designate another. The human mind is the only mind capable of thinking metaphorically, and our language and culture are full of metaphors, wherever you look: 'sky-scrapers', 'time flies', 'the world is a stage'.

Using metaphors in your selling is a great way to describe something so that your buyer gets it immediately; it removes a level of mental calculation and presents the problem as something the buyer can easily relate to.

A recent client described their technology as 'an engine'. Another described their software as 'a house' with different rooms with different functions. Both are effective, easily understood descriptions for rather complex bits of technology.

When coming up with your metaphor, try thinking about which characteristics of your offer would easily translate into a metaphor, and how this might relate to your buyer's needs.

TRY THIS:
Are you able to describe your product or offer in terms of something more familiar to your buyer?

Is your consultancy going to 'send a rocket' through their organisation?

TOOL 27: SPICE IT UP

When my sales writing was assessed, energy was one of the key attributes that was identified – but how in reality do you add energy? One solution is to pepper your sales writing with adjectives and adverbs.

Adjectives typically refer to the state of something, e.g. fast, clever.

Adverbs modify verbs, adjectives and other adverbs, e.g. incredibly, rapidly, cleverly, very.

Examples for your sales writing:
- our *exciting* launch
- the *escalating* need for ...
- I'm *extremely* keen to chat regarding ...
- *continual* improvement
- *futuristic* consultancy
- the *clever* software.

Your reader wants to be moved and wants to know why you care. Adjectives work wonders at injecting energy into your email, press release, pitch – or indeed any piece of writing.

Using adjectives and adverbs also adds urgency to your writing – a central hot button in decision-making.

To speed up your sales communications, you might also use words that literally mean 'quick', 'short' and 'simple':
- this *fast* test
- a *short* introduction
- this *snippet* of content.

The quicker buyers are able to read your communications, without tripping up over the words, the more urgent your pitch will seem. But that's not the only way to increase urgency. You can also add words with emotional appeal, such as: *in-demand*, *cutting-edge*, *running-out*, *dwindling*, *increasing* ...

Be cautious: overuse these words and your communication will feel gimmicky and fake. Use them sparingly and wisely and you'll instantly bolster emotional appeal.

TRY THIS:
Before you construct your sales messages, think about how and where you could add energy and urgency to your sentences. Using the

26

The N

PRODUCT FEATURE

e.g. TECHNOLOGY

etaphor

THE METAPHOR

e.g. ENGINE

27

SPICE IT

e.g. exciting

e.g.

LAUNCH

concrete language of Tool 25, write down your key product features.
And then write down some adjectives or adverbs that would be most
suitable to spice these up. Select from these to write your full sentences.

TIRED OLD EMAIL

Email – it's just about hanging on as an effective sales medium to reach our buyers. Email open rates have fallen rapidly and response rates too.

Whilst social platforms are boasting of higher rates of 'engagement', email is still an effective medium of choice for many buyers, and offers you the opportunity to use many of the tools in this section. Used effectively, the subject box and the body copy can help you generate likeability and generate more clicks that lead to the all-important 'yes, please'.

TOOL 28: DO, DOING, DONE

There are lots of different emails you may need to write in your sales career and none is easy to make compelling, not least the sales email introducing your product from cold.

For this email, the 'Do, Doing, Done' formula is a handy tool. It enables you to use much of the information you have acquired in previous tools and include as many emotional hot buttons as possible.

Do – what you want to do

Your opening line is potentially all the buyer is going to read, so this important sentence must be well thought through.

Writer Barnaby Conrad was very aware of the importance of the opening line when he said: 'Hone your opening words, for just as stories aren't written but rewritten, so should beginnings be written and rewritten. Look at your opening and ask yourself, "If I were reading this, would I be intrigued enough to go on?"'

In the first line of your email, tell them what you want to do. Get straight to the point. Don't waste time with false niceties and meaningless 'how are you's.

Like this:
'Our tool enables risk prevention, which I feel could be beneficial for your company, with your current expansion plans and associated safety concerns.'

Or this:
'A brief note to check if our keynotes will be a useful fit for any events you're running during 2016.'

Doing – what you're doing

What you say in your doing sentence or short paragraph should be the result of Tools 16–18, The Hook, The Stretch or The Magnify.

This needs to be short, simple, get immediately to the point and tell the buyer what they need to know in relation to their challenges, their big picture and/or their personal goals. It needs to pack a punch and resonate immediately.

Like this:
'We're a highly Google-optimised job board for senior executives and our most recent statistics reveal we have 531,496 registered professionals actively seeking new careers in finance.'

Or this:
'Our research will prove you're communicating to the people that matter. And our reports will give you a true understanding of your target audience, making your PR much more effective.'

Done – what you've done

This is your opportunity to home in on a moment in time, use Tool 22, The Reality Check, and the emotional hot button of social pressure. What else have you done recently that would be of interest?

28

DO, DOING DONE.

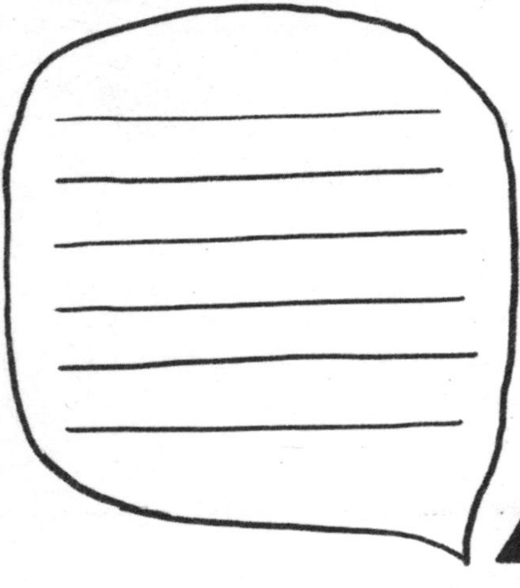

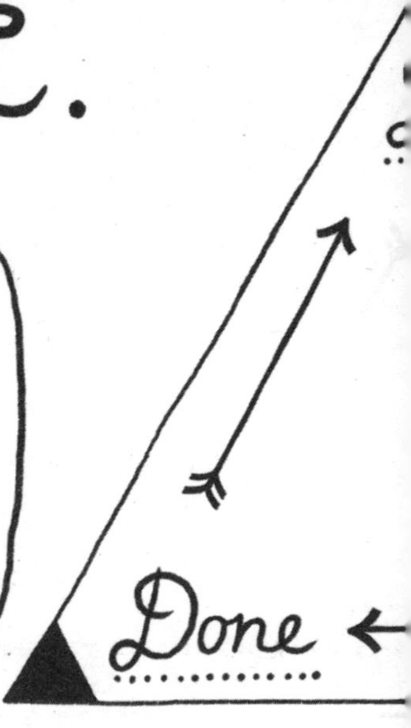

Doing

Like this:
'Most recently we've enabled Dillons & Miller to transition to mobile commerce.'

Another email framework enabling you to use the Story Star and *what* and *why* effectively is 'what, how, why'. If you're a little further along in the sale, or perhaps communicating with an existing client, this 'what, how, why' structure works well.

Communicate:
What you want to do;
How you're going to do it;
Why it's important.

Like this:
'I'd like to offer you a demo of our research tool.'

'I'll share a quick form for you to tell me what functions would be most useful.'

'This will give you a clear idea of the tool's scope, and allow you to gather useful feedback from your team on useful applications at XYZ.'

TRY THIS:
Write your sales email following the 'Do, Doing, Done' structure. Use Tools 5–13 to collate and identify the information you need to include.

TOOL 29: THE KILLER SUBJECT LINE

In advertising, the headline has always been hugely significant – it dictates the reader's first impression, their instantaneous decision and their emotional shortcut to the yes or no.

David Ogilvy rightly noted that 'On average five times as many people read the headline as the body copy. It follows that unless your headline sells your product, you have wasted 90 per cent of your money'.

In sales too, you have the opportunity to make the same impact through the headline in your email's subject box and considerably improve open rates.

If your message has impact at this stage, then you're encouraging the reader's mind to accept the sales message. As your email drops into an overflowing inbox, your business-to-business buyer decides whether they like you and what you're saying, whether what you're selling is relevant to them and, most importantly, whether they're going to delete you or read on – a catalogue of instantaneous decisions, based on a few simple words.

Every day, my own inbox is filled with highly deletable subjects like:
- 'Helen, get 10 per cent off' (no thanks, you're competing against a hundred similar offers)
- 'December Newsletter' (going to give that one a major swerve!)
- 'Free trial of ABC Software' (no time, sorry – and I'm not at all emotionally sold here).

If you get the subject box right, you will hook your reader from the outset, get your offer read, and sell your product far more often.

Here are some dos:

Be about them
No one cares you've just launched a new hotel or new advertising platform. All the reader cares about is what's in it for them. Try changing a subject like 'Investor relations services' into 'Communicating with your investors'– and watch your response rate rise.

Use the word *you*. We all care about ourselves, our jobs and our successes. The subject needs to be aimed squarely at your recipient and 'you' and 'your' are hugely powerful words. For example, change 'Monitoring software' to 'What about your site?' Change 'Great gardening tips' to 'Your garden = the Mediterranean'. Another great example I saw recently was 'Are you normal?'

29

THE KILLER SUBJECT LINE

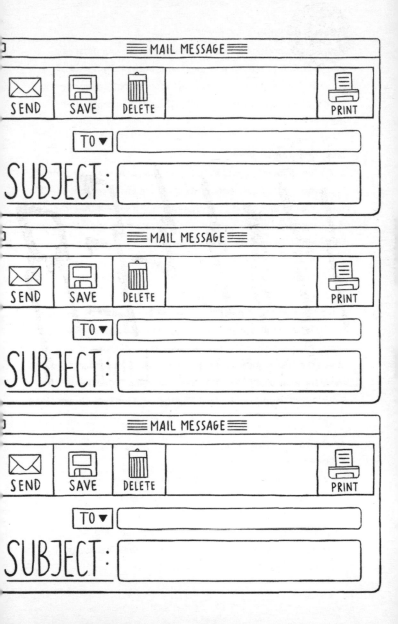

Look into the future

How can you position your product so it propels your prospect into the future? Appealing to the buyer's desire to be ahead of the curve will pique interest and appeal to the hot button of urgency. 'An early heads up' was a great subject I spotted recently that made me click!

Imply rapid consumption

Imply the content is going to be quick to consume – you've done the hard work for them. No one wants to read reams of content and if they have multiple tasks to do that morning a subject that implies a 'quick overview' or a 'snippet of content' is far more appealing than something that implies time to digest.

Add momentum

There are various stages of a sell when you may need to use the subject box wisely. To prospect, of course, but another crucial time is following an initial meeting when you're sending over your thoughts on working together or even the full proposal of business. This is the opportunity to add momentum into your subject box and move the relationship along. Rather than using 'Proposal', use the subject 'Next steps', or 'Working together', and lead your buyer along the sales journey.

And here are some don'ts:

- Don't sell in the subject box.
- Don't use trickery. Your subject box must relate to your message. A gimmicky, unrelated subject will only cause resentment.
- Never use caps lock, it just looks like you're shouting.
- Never use exclamation marks or ellipses – they look too pushy and gimmicky.

TRY THIS:
Write a subject line for your email based on the tips above or so that it fulfils one of these three criteria:
- use the word *you* or *your*
- imply rapid consumption
- add momentum.

TOOL 30: THE SQUEEZE

Email may still be our communication tool of choice in the workplace but it's clinging on for dear life. Simpler, less wordy, instant, free and ultimately smarter communication apps are spilling over from our social into our professional life.

For example, LinkedIn, Twitter, Facebook and WhatsApp are all hot on email's heels.

WhatsApp is an instant messenger app that allows us to communicate with anyone for free and to create friendship, interest and, increasingly, professional groups. Along with the other similar technologies, it's quickly taking up ground once reserved by email.

Using WhatsApp, in just a few words we can get the information we need, and decide 'yes' or 'no' to a whole host of questions – from meeting friends to going on a date and, soon enough, deciding whether or not to meet a salesperson and discuss their product.

So let's imagine we were writing to sell on WhatsApp. What would or could you say in those few lines?

If I were selling sales development, it would be simple: 'We focus on the mind, upskilling sellers and giving them the mental tools to excite, persuade and close more sales, more often.'

Or for a future-focused leadership-development firm: 'The content of our workshops is about your future and will educate and upskill your leaders to navigate what's next.'

30

'THE SQUEEZE'

08:45 ✓✓

TRY THIS:
Imagine you have to send a sales message on WhatsApp. A condensed version of the classic elevator pitch as described above.

What would you write?

Test Yourself
Now you've read how to construct a good email pitch, and gained a feel for the structure and content that generates interest, test yourself by looking at the following emails and WhatsApp messages, and identifying:
- the 'Do, Doing, Done' or the 'what, how, why' structure
- the use of emotional hot buttons (refer to the PBI for a reminder about these)
- a strong subject line
- the story (who, what, how, why, when, where)
- the hook (about them).

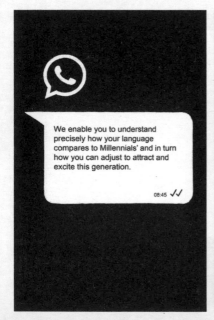

```
┌─────────────────────────────────────────────────────────┐
│ □                    ≡ MAIL MESSAGE ≡                     │
├─────────────────────────────────────────────────────────┤
│ ┌────┐ ┌────┐ ┌────┐                            ┌────┐   │
│ │ ✉  │ │ 💾 │ │ 🗑  │                            │ 🖨  │   │
│ │SEND│ │SAVE│ │DELETE│                           │PRINT│  │
│ └────┘ └────┘ └────┘                            └────┘   │
│        ┌──────┐┌──────────────────────────────────────┐  │
│        │ TO ▼ ││                                      │  │
│        └──────┘└──────────────────────────────────────┘  │
│   SUBJECT: ┌──────────────────────────────────────────┐  │
│            │ Reaching self-directed investors         │  │
│            └──────────────────────────────────────────┘  │
```

Hi Mary,

It would be great to get some time in to chat with you regarding developments here at ▇▇▇▇ that are specifically relevant for ▇▇▇▇.

The recent and continuing rise of self-directed investment has created new opportunities for wealth management and we've a number of opportunities across print, events and mobile that enable you to reach our high net-worth active-investor audience.

Recently, ▇▇▇▇, looking to secure more face-to-face time with active investors, ran a breakfast at our HQ ▇▇▇▇

Do let me know a good time to chat – it would be great to hear about your plans for 2016.

Best regards

Helen

This will allow you to see these structures in action, and to learn how you might apply them in your own sales communications. Not every email or Whatsapp message contains all the elements – the next step is to identify where they could be made better!

KEEP YOURSELF IN CHECK

With the best will in the world, it's easy to veer off course when communicating your sell, and to resort to an egocentric, rational-heavy sell.

What you need is an internal mental coach keeping you empathetic *and* making sure you keep your knowledge at the centre of the emotional sell. Tools 31 and 32 are two checks you can use to keep yourself on track.

TOOL 31: THE THEM SCALE

The recipient is scanning your communication with one thing in mind: 'What's in it for me?' It's all too easy to sway towards communication that forgets this and focuses on you and your product – unless that is, you keep yourself in check.

Using Tool 31, at one end of the scale, imagine we have sales communication that is utterly about you. It's egocentric, product-heavy, highly ignorable sales garbage. But at the other end there is communication that is about the recipient. It takes into account their needs, desires, goals and hot buttons, and the hook is resonant and empathetic.

TRY THIS:
Each time you write a piece of communication to your client – a pitch, an email, a proposal – take time to review it using the Them Scale, with your buyer in mind.

What does your communication look like? Where in the scale does your communication sit? How much is it about them, versus about you?

Too much about you, and you'll have to rethink it. And too much about them, you'll have to ask: have you made it clear what you do?

TOOL 32: THE EMOTIONAL SCALE

We know that likeability is one of the key emotional hot buttons that we can use when selling. This can be reinforced by the style of our communication, and many of the **to think** tools will help with this. But we must still make sure we're using other hot buttons, such as social pressure or scarcity as and when appropriate.

At one end of the scale we have sales communication that is emotionally void, and at the other, sales communication overflowing with emotion and lacking in argument.

TRY THIS:
Assess your communication for emotional resonance. Identify the hot buttons, look for purpose and use this scale.

Also look for the rational story – is your argument clear, empathetic and strong?

Use this tool to ensure you hit the middle ground.

THE POWER OF PICTURES

Using the right words in the right order, at the right time, is essential to any great selling activity. But there is something that trumps the effectiveness of words: directly using visuals in your selling.

Language, however concrete, is always much harder for the brain to process than images; the brain processes visuals as much as 60,000 times faster than text. According to a phenomenon known as the

31

THE »THEM« SCALE

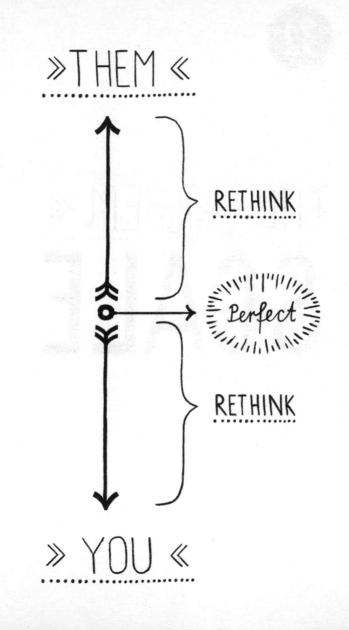

32

THE EMOTIONAL
SCALE

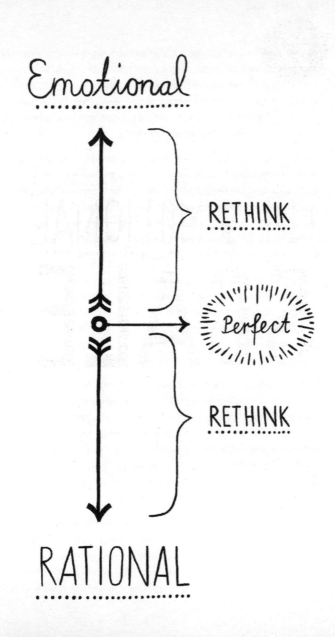

picture superiority effect, we are also six times more likely to remember a picture rather than words seventy-two hours later. Using words and pictures together enhances this impact further, and consolidates the facts you're trying to communicate. Visuals also appeal to our more emotional right brain. This is important to know when we're looking to get noticed and remembered with our selling.

Leonardo da Vinci was an advocate for the power of drawing rather than over-describing. He believed that using too many words to explain things just confuses the audience: 'for the more thoroughly you describe, the more you will confuse the mind of the reader and the more you will prevent him from a knowledge of the thing described: it is therefore necessary to draw as well as to describe ... I advise you not to trouble with words unless you are speaking to a blind man.'

Using pictures in your selling will prevent the confusion that can occur when we try to explain the complex. By visually depicting what you're offering, you will remove potential ambiguity and automatically make it very clear what you're trying to explain. You'll be able to visualise the right bits of your story, avoid any unwanted jargon and achieve the holy grail of sales communication: the buyer gets it.

There's a common misconception that by using visuals you'll make your sell too simple. But the real goal of creating a visual representation of your sell is not to over-simplify but to make what you're trying to say visible. This doesn't necessarily mean producing a picture worthy of Leonardo da Vinci himself. As powerful as a full-blown painting is, a sketch or doodle using visuals that are immediately recognisable, and which everyone can understand, is what you need in your selling.

Precognitive visuals are ideal. These are very simple images like a thumbs-up to mean 'good' and a heart to mean 'love'. These images are worked on by the unconscious long before our conscious mind catches up. They don't involve much mental effort to understand and, as such, are a useful aid when visualising your sell. Whether your sell

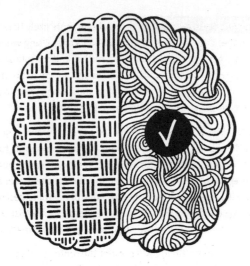

demands a simple picture or an elaborate image of the scenario in mind will depend on the audience's knowledge of the subject.

As with words, you must have the buyer in mind when you create your visuals. Ask yourself: 'What do they need to see to get this?'

When we look at a visual, we first see it and mentally process it – and then immediately imagine ourselves in that scenario. We'll then look to the words for extra clarity. When constructing a visual, therefore, we must be as empathetic as in our writing. Use Tool 14 here to get yourself into the mind of the buyer and ask yourself, 'What would they like to see?', 'How can I make sure the buyer sees themselves and then wants my product?'

I regularly use visuals in my selling. I start with a pen in hand and literally sketch what it is I'm trying to sell. To kick-start using visuals in your selling, here are two visual techniques: Tool 33, Draw It: Three Steps, and Tool 34, Draw It: Them. Both techniques help the buyer to see themselves and their situation more readily.

TOOL 33: DRAW IT: THREE STEPS

We've already discussed the usefulness of dividing a sell into three steps, and this three-step process is perfectly suited to being accompanied by a visual representation to add further clarity.

You can use visuals in this way when selling face-to-face, by just picking up your pen and drawing. Or if you work closely with a designer, you can create digital images to be used online and across pitch documents, social media and emails.

- Start by thinking of your three-step process – one that includes an input, a process and an output.
- Now illustrate those stages: the first visual, on the far left, should be the buyer's current situation.
- In the centre, you should visualise 'how you help'.
- And on the far right, visualise their 'improved scenario', after you've been involved.

This structure also creates a visual 'flow' from left to right, a sense of movement that mirrors the idea of progress and development that you are offering your buyer. Once you have drawn this 'flow', add words that will bolster the effectiveness of the images.

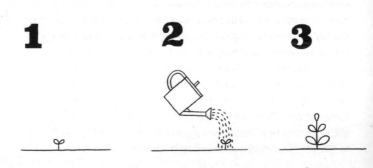

In my example, a three-step sell is playfully illustrated by images of growth. The first step is planting a seed (your client as a small business), the second step is using a watering can to develop the seed (you, the facilitator of growth), and finally we have the growth of the plant (the output or end result – thanks to you).

TRY THIS:

Look back at Tool 24, Three Steps, to remind yourself that an effective sell has a beginning, a middle and an end. It's this structure that enables the recipient to see how your product or service takes them from where they are now to where they want to be. Now use the space provided in Tool 33 to visualise those three stages of your sell, using simple line drawings.

Think about how this could be reproduced digitally, and how it might form the first page of a proposal or create the main image on a web page for a prospecting campaign.

TOOL 34: DRAW IT: THEM

Your buyer is looking at the image you've created, trying to imagine precisely how this relates to them. By creating an image that simply and clearly depicts the buyer and placing it centrally in your illustration, you immediately up the empathy levels.

Creating a visual like this means that you can also jump directly to the right bit of the story and demonstrate what, in sales, we call 'situational fluency'. This means being able to speak with ease about your buyer's current situation – something you should be able to do already if you have completed the ABI. To demonstrate situational fluency in the context of a face-to-face meeting, you need to know which bit of your sell is most enticing to the buyer, adjusting your idea based on the conversation you're having. Rather than selling them everything you've got, or starting from the beginning, you can use a visual to jump directly to the bit of your story that is right for them. If they are only interested

DRAW IT
≫3 Steps≪

1

CURRENT SCENARIO

2
HO

OU HELP

IMPROVED SCENARIO

DRAW IT:

≫ THEM ≪

in your sponsorship opportunities and not the wider advertising remit, for example, then visualise just this opportunity.

Think of your buyer as the centre of this visual; around them, draw the visible benefits of using your product. Again, use words in conjunction with the visuals to up the impact and the clarity.

In my examples, you will see the buyer is represented by a circle for simplicity. In your scenario, you may choose any shape you like. Again, precognitive visuals are good here, like a stick man, a brain, a head, an arrow or even the outline of a computer.

TRY THIS:

Imagine your buyer at the centre of the picture. Draw your product or service around them. How exactly do you support them, bolster their current position and catapult them into the future? How can you symbolise this using precognitive visuals?

The important thing in using visuals is to increase empathy. Play with using visuals for a while until you feel confident.

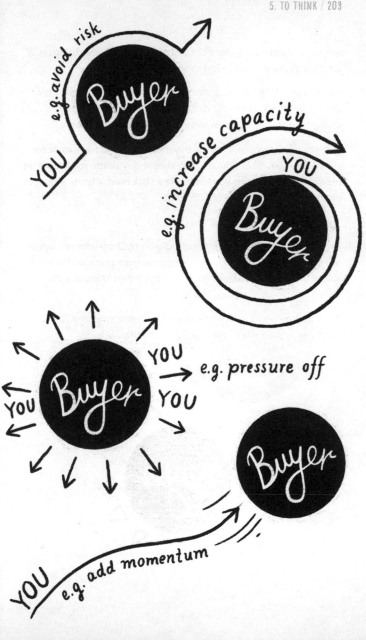

'To

improve,

'SHE KNOWS THERE'S NO
SUCCESS LIKE FAILURE.
AND THAT FAILURE'S NO
SUCCESS AT ALL.' BOB DYLAN

6

Tools 35–46 will help you:

- *recognise, embrace and learn from your mistakes*

- *overcome your mindless approach to progress and accept a more flexible approach to success*

- *use and perfect your very own creating mind to enhance the impact of your selling.*

At this stage, Tools 1–34 have enabled you to hold reality still long enough for you to recognise your buyer's big picture and granular reality. You have extended your knowledge beyond organisational drivers to include personal drivers, and recognised the increasing role of meaning (the *why*) in decision-making. By synthesising all the information at your disposal you have been able to position and package your product so that your sales story really hits home with your buyer.

But you're not finished yet. Just when you think you've nailed it, sooner or later you'll be saying the same thing as everyone else, and your sell will have lost its impact altogether. Frustratingly, you'll be saying the right things, but your interpretation – your hook – will have become utterly ignorable.

Why? Because it will have lost its refreshing uniqueness. The complete knowledge you acquired in the ABI meant you were able to create a sell to enliven your buyer's mind, encouraging them to receive your sales message. But sooner or later, this impact will fade, competitors will catch up and your unique style will become the mainstream. This is one of the major hazards in sales. Sales-hungry companies develop sales messaging and hungry sellers take it to market. But then they mindlessly fail to review this for months, sometimes years, on end. This inevitably results in lack of interest, shrinking response rates and a reduction in sales. In other words, the sales approach is failing.

On top of this, you may not yet have quite interpreted your raw materials right. You have all the knowledge and have diligently synthesised this into what you feel is compelling communication, but, unless you are actually the buyer, it is very difficult to know what their real reaction will be. Result: another failing sales approach.

But all is not lost. These kinds of challenges are to be expected in all selling activity and should be accepted as important stages of improvement. This is something that experienced and confident sellers recognise and embrace. They are fully aware that their selling is far from a static activity, that it is very much a dynamic process, frequently turbulent, with highs and lows, successes and failures in equal measure.

Contrary to what you may believe, misdirection and mistakes are an essential part of successful selling. Selling without mistakes can only ever be mediocre and cannot stand the test of time. Improving effectively involves embracing the lows, the mistakes and the dips in success. It's the downs that feed far greater ups, because information gathered from these troughs enables sellers to be clearer on how to improve impact next time – which is where you can use your imagination, your inherent creative skill.

To improve, then, involves two vital human mechanisms: the drive to be continually learning, and our natural creative abilities.

BECOME A MISTAKE EXPERT

The problem we face with this undulating approach to success is that our ingrained mental preference is for a more linear approach to progress. We feel more comfortable following a straight path than one with dips, setbacks and hurdles. Ellen Langer calls this our ingrained 'outcome orientation', which, in our mindless state, is difficult to let go.

Langer claims that this starts in school, with our first experiences in education; we are taught to be concerned with value and look towards goals, the successful end point, rather than conquering the process by which these goals are methodically and painstakingly achieved. Our first memories of achievement are framed around delivery of a desired outcome resulting in a reward (i.e. good test result first time round = the 'right' sort of intelligence) with few second chances and limited opportunity to change our position by learning from mistakes. Langer elaborates: 'this single-minded pursuit of one outcome or another, from tying shoelaces to getting into Harvard, makes it difficult to have a mindful attitude about life.'

This goal orientation has become a deeply entrenched mindset, both on an individual level and as the overriding standpoint adopted by corporations. Unfortunately, speed and efficiency are the core values of this approach and we have been programmed to feel uncomfortable with, or even afraid of, non-linear progress involving failure.

The entire skill of selling is best completed in this non-linear fashion. The best sellers have learnt to overcome this mindset and embrace mistakes. Rather than 'Can I do it?', Langer suggests we ask ourselves 'How do I do it?', which forces us to attend mindfully to each step of the learning process. It's not a case of 'If this fails then I'm a failure'; it should be 'If this fails I'll tweak that bit – and try again.' This is the mental standpoint of the greatest sales professionals.

This is a form of process philosophy, which recognises that all activity is a process. To achieve this in our selling, we must begin a shift from a linear, mindless approach and instead adopt a 'processist' approach, understanding the need for continual evolution and change. In our selling process, there will be no failure, just ineffective options which we can learn from and improve on to magnify success.

✗
OUTCOME ORIENTATION

✓
PROCESS ORIENTATION

We don't like to think that good things stem from mistakes, but the fact is that we owe a huge debt to our mistakes – we learn more, much more, from these than from successes. And the more mistakes we make, the more we learn. As ad man Claude Hopkins noted: 'The man who does two or three times the work of another learns two or three times as much. He makes more mistakes and more successes and learns from both.'

Daniel C. Dennett, present-day philosopher and self-confessed mistake-maker, suggests that we should all be making lots of 'good mistakes', and learning from these all along the way. It's these good mistakes that light the way forward: 'mistakes are not just opportunities for learning, they are, in an important sense, the only opportunity for learning and making something truly new.'

The positive impact of mistakes forms the basis of what psychologist B. F. Skinner called 'reinforcement learning'. In the longer term, mistakes and their resulting improvement are stored in the memory in your Feeler, ensuring that you won't make them again in a hurry.

The art of making good mistakes is to become a master of your own mistakes and to turn them over in your mind.

Learning like this is a continual process, whilst knowledge is a stockpile, a static accumulation. In sales it's as important to learn continually from mistakes as it is to know some things for certain.

Trying, failing and then learning from your own experience is far superior to reading about how to do something in any sales textbook. Hopkins was a fan of this 'school of experience' and recognised how difficult it is to learn salesmanship: 'I have read some of those courses. They were so misleading, so impractical, that they exasperated me. Once a man brought me from a great technical school their course in advertising and asked me how to improve it. When I read it I said, "Burn it. You have no right to occupy a young man's most impressive years, most precious years, with rot like that." If he spends four years to learn such theories, he will spend a dozen years to unlearn them.'

The teachings in this book, the tools and theory, are built on the foundation of many mistakes, which all revealed and reinforced what is right and what is certain. The tools are shortcuts for you to reach the same level of understanding, but the important thing is to continue to make your own mistakes, and reach conclusions via your own experience.

As well as learning from mistakes, it is crucial to learn from what works and to repeat the winners. Your audience is changing all the time and you must hold on to and exploit what generates the right response.

One great way to do this is to keep a file of successful language, images and campaigns, either yours or other people's. Source them from other industries too. Some of the greatest ideas I have had have been a version of something I've seen work really well elsewhere.

TOOL 35: THE SHARK'S TEETH

The foundation of all scientific discovery – from day-to-day experiments through to some of the greatest discoveries of all time – involves an educated guess by an experienced scientist with a base of knowledge. This is the hypothesis. This is then followed by an experiment and delivery of the findings, which can often be unexpected and lead to a rethink, a refocus and a redo. This is the basis of trial and error, and without it, the experiment would get nowhere and we would learn nothing. Much of the best science is yet to progress beyond this very stage, still working towards perfection. And selling is the same.

New and innovative thinking will *always* end in a certain number of mistakes – but you'll be achieving much more than your risk-averse peers. Becoming a master of mistake-making is the key to making progress in sales.

You can think of the ideal sales journey as shaped like a shark's teeth, with highs and lows all along the process.

TRY THIS:
For your next sales project, after you have gathered all the knowledge you need and interpreted your sell, share this with others. Track the response, and learn from the reasons for rejection. Put simply – gather results, learn from them – and improve.

Or think about a project when you achieved great success in the face of adversity. How did you learn from the negative? How did it enhance your process?

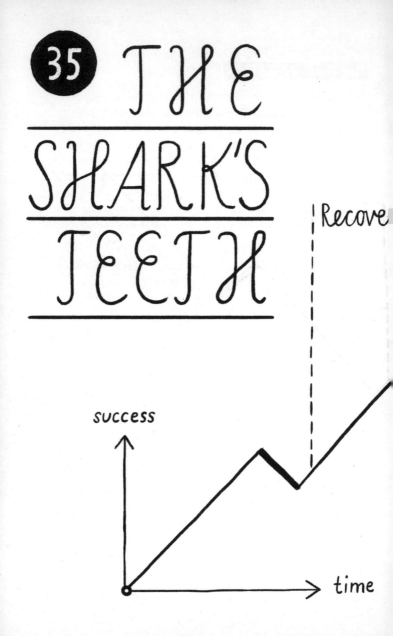

35 THE SHARK'S TEETH

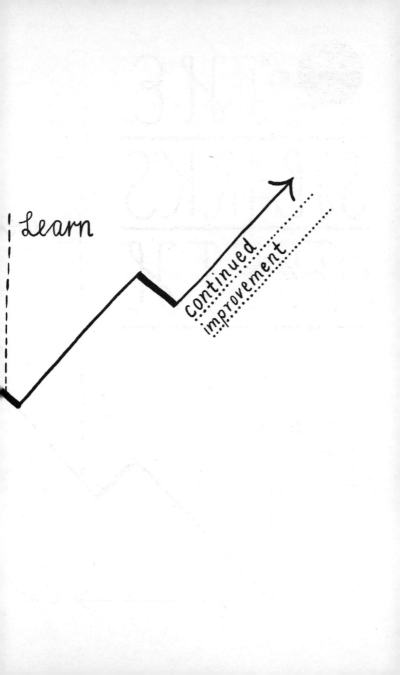

TOOL 36: THE COIL

The fact is, we very rarely, if ever, produce our best work on the first attempt, and your best selling is like this – it will take time and several drafts until you reach the right model. Each attempt is necessary, and each attempt adds to the final result. But it will take several attempts to achieve perfection.

Think about each sales attempt like a coil with three equal-sized loops – this will force you to complete the project at least three times. The first attempt is about getting your thoughts out of your Thinker and on to paper, logging them so they can be manipulated and improved. This stage is only likely to produce a basic first draft – something to be crumpled up and reworked in the next draft. The second attempt will be an improvement and the third will produce perfection – or close enough.

To excel with your sales messaging and communication, don't aim to finalise important projects on the first attempt. Expect to stretch the number of times you complete the project. The magic number seems to be at least three times. And leaving a decent amount of time between each attempt also helps.

At each stage of the cycle, you improve and perfect.

TRY THIS:
When creating your sell, use this coil model to take the pressure off your first attempt. You attempt something, then you improve on it and, by the third try, you perfect it. Between each attempt, give yourself time to gather the facts and think about what you want to create and communicate.

UP THE CREATIVE ANTE

Using the latest technology, we're increasingly able to measure not only how many times our messages are read and shared, but where they're read, when and on what device. It's easy to see which messages and campaign styles are working and which ones aren't, and there are now hundreds of 'observational' technologies offering their services to sales teams. This data is useful but shouldn't be treated as an end in and of itself, rather as the *means* to an end.

It's important to recognise this. Some sales and marketing-focused organisations are placing far too much emphasis on this data, too concerned with the facts and not enough with learning from them to deliver game-changing ideas.

The more we know, the more we end up just sounding like everyone else. After all, doing it mathematically means everyone is doing it the same way, leading to buyer boredom like never before.

In this climate of buyer apathy, we can use this data and our knowledge to stir up the creativity of our selling and make the all-important impact. Technology can assist us with this goal, but it mustn't take control.

Psychologist William James was always more interested in what he called 'the unscientific half of existence', the bit that reminds us that science is in fact incomplete. Truly successful selling contains this unscientific edge and seeks to create a fresh and innovative style and delivery.

Playing it safe is no longer playing it smart. The only way to stand out is to up the creative ante.

YOU ARE CREATIVE

Perhaps when you think of creativity you don't think it's relevant to your role, and that being creative should be reserved instead for the arty or the gifted. This couldn't be further from the truth.

BRIEF

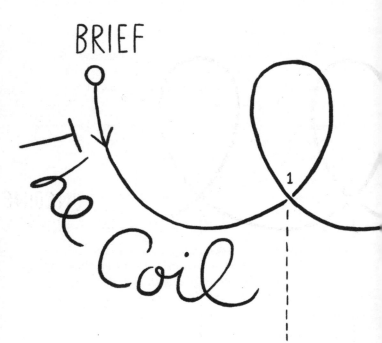

The Coil

1

ATTEMPT

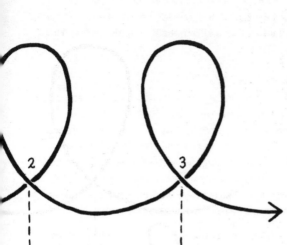

2

3

ONGOING
SUCCESS

IMPROVE   PERFECT

Every time you modify a behaviour or make up a new recipe or persuade your daughter, brother or spouse to see things your way – you are being creative. Architects are creative when they squeeze an extra room into a tiny plot of land. Farmers are creative when they diversify crops in response to climate change. Your teacher was incredibly creative when she found a new way to finally teach you the seven times table.

Creative 'types' create good ideas because we are all capable of creating good ideas. This is what our minds, with our Feeler and our Thinker, unconscious and conscious thoughts, intuitive and working memories, were made for.

All About the Sale
What is important is that creativity in sales has still got to be about selling more. How long does it take until your sell, your story, your method of delivery has become boring? Two months? Maybe less. Your hook (Tool 16) will need refreshing, and your POV (Tool 20), which was once so surprising and challenging, will need rethinking. It's the creative mind that translates your point of view into compelling and unique solutions that will provoke and excite your buyer. Thinking of new ways to sell old stuff isn't just a nice skill to have, it's an essential skill.

At a recent Cannes Lions International Festival of Creativity, sales and profit took centre stage in their description of this sometimes rather vague activity: 'creativity which has shown a measurable and proven impact on a client's business – creativity that affects consumer behaviour, brand equity, sales and, where identifiable, profit'.

You can describe creativity in sales as a new way of doing something, which in turn generates a greater impact and yields a greater return. Thinking creatively will help you sell more.

THE THREE Ps FOR THE CREATING MIND

We all have the capability to be creative, and to bring fresh ideas and exciting innovations to our work – no matter what our job title is.

Institutions can be afraid of creative endeavour, but it's important to remember that the boss isn't always right. At Disney, ideas are encouraged to come from the floor, says Peter Rummell, former chairman of Imagineering at Disney: 'I think one of the major lessons I learnt was that despite the hierarchy of an organization, an idea can come from anywhere. If you're the top guy, that doesn't mean you have a great idea; doesn't mean you have the best idea; doesn't mean you're going to be the most valuable person in the process.' That 'best idea' could be anyone's – it could be yours!

The first step in generating good ideas, then, is taking personal responsibility. The people who have the most ideas interpret their own world and don't just accept other people's interpretations.

In *Five Minds for the Future*, Howard Gardner describes the creating mind as 'able to go beyond existing knowledge and synthesis to pose new questions, offer new solutions, fashion works that stretch existing genres or configure new ones'. Discovering new ways to do old things is crucial for sellers at any level, and so we must work to find ways of fostering our creating mind.

Creativity requires a certain amount of both clear direction and utter chaos in order to result in exciting ideas. Set the parameters too tight and the best ideas will never come, but don't give yourself any guidelines at all and you'll fail to land on the right insight and your ideas will spiral out of control.

To help master these two crucial attitudes and to hone your creativity, I have identified three crucial steps to achieving that 'aha!' moment of a unique sales idea:

- prepare
- play
- ponder.

Within the structure of these three steps, you'll have the flexibility to let your creating mind explore and discover. As we have seen, the right hemisphere in our thinking brain has the tendency to be more creative. The neurons have longer pathways, making unassociated patterns easier to see, and allowing a greater grasp of the big picture. Evidence suggests that those with higher levels of right-brain activity solve problems with imaginative insight far more often. Within each step are tools that will encourage your right brain to think creatively, make those connections and arrive at that light-bulb moment.

1. PREPARE

Effective preparation means putting in the ground work. Before you can generate the most exciting or creative insights, you need a well-informed Feeler and a clear big-picture view of all associated variables. Immerse yourself in your genre, make all the mistakes, and consciously fill your mind with information. People who have the best ideas, most often, have them because they work the hardest. There are no short cuts. The more knowledge you have of your subject, the more creative you are able to be.

David Ogilvy was a firm believer in the importance of preparation: 'Big ideas come from the unconscious. This is true in art, in science and in advertising. But the unconscious has to be well informed. Or the idea will be irrelevant.'

To fully prepare, you must also tell your mind what it needs to work on. To enable your Thinker to identify the right patterns and land on the insight, you must give a clear brief, just as you would to a creative agency. It's best to keep these briefs simple and succinct, and give yourself one challenge to solve at a time.

TOOL 37: THE SPIDER BRIEF

The Spider Brief is a way of tackling a large creative task, breaking it down into manageable chunks that won't overwhelm your Thinker.

The central brief might be, for example, 'How do we sell more fitness classes to mums?' This central question is hard for your mind to compute; there are countless solutions and no clear patterns can be uncovered. The spider brief allows you to break this question into sub-briefs like:

- What exercises are more time-consuming for mums?
- What could we offer mums that they can't do at home?

When writing this book, I faced hundreds of creative challenges. How should I best describe this theory? How should this tool be illustrated? Trying to tackle them as a lump would have been hopeless. I had to brief myself, one small challenge at a time.

TRY THIS:
What are you trying to achieve? Write your core challenge in the central circle, the body of the spider. For example, 'How do we generate meetings with CEO's?'

Now break out from this central question and be more specific with your brief. What other questions do you need to answer? What other headlines will lead to smaller pieces of important insight? For example, 'What is keeping CEOs awake at night?' 'What do we do that is utterly unique, and how do I package this unique feature so CEOs can access it?'

Answer these smaller briefs and they will answer the bigger brief for you.

TOOL 38: SKETCH YOUR BRIEF

In order to use your Thinker effectively, you need to help it hold as much information as possible, to allow patterns to be found. But as we have already discovered, your Thinker's working memory can only hold three to five pieces of information at a time.

As we discussed when examining the power of pictures to sell (Tools 33 and 34), sketching your brief will allow you to visualise your information by getting it down on paper, which in turn gives your working memory more space to bring things in from your Feeler and land on the right insight more readily.

37

THE
SPIDER
BRIEF

38

Sketch yo

You could draw what you want to achieve, the ideal end goal prompted by the brief; this will allow your Thinker to focus on how you will get there.

Or you could sketch your buyer in their current situation; this will remove large chunks of basic information from your Thinker and enable it to work with other crucial facts to find an alternative. If you're selling a tool that automates their accounting procedure, let's say, then draw them struggling with multiple devices and see what your brain comes up with whilst looking at the image in front of you.

Drawing your brief also engages your creative right brain, helping you see the big picture more readily.

TRY THIS:
Grab a pen and sketch your goal, or your buyer's current situation without you. Get this information out of your Thinker and use this sketch as a reference point whilst working through the problem.

TOOL 39: ACCESS THE FEELER: THREE THINGS

When attempting to land on the right insight, our Feeler will often feed the information to our Thinker, we'll recognise a pattern and come up with an idea quickly. These are your 'gut-reaction' ideas, often discarded or forgotten too quickly.

Following the brief to yourself, set your first thoughts down on paper quickly, as these can often be very useful initial ideas. Particularly if your brief was clear.

I have heard this referred to as 'holding the idea lightly'. These quick thoughts won't necessarily be the final insight but they're very useful to have noted down none the less. You will be able to expand them, reject them and play with them later, and they are a way of avoiding the paralysing feeling that your first idea must be the best.

TRY THIS:
Following on from Tools 37 and 38, what are the first three things that come into your mind? What are your initial ideas? Jot these down, whatever they are.

2. PLAY

Now you have all the information you need, you have briefed yourself and sketched your brief – but the ideas still aren't coming. You need to move away from rigid thinking, start to draw on your packed Feeler and allow your Thinker to play. The most creative people on the planet are fully aware that extracting the best ideas means playing with them first, stretching their meaning and exploring all the options.

TOOL 40: UNLIMITED BUDGET

We are plagued by the idea that we are trapped by forces outside our control, like lack of budget, time or resources. This sense of confinement is a big sap on creative energies and restricts our view of the impact we can make.

Imagine instead that there are no limits and you have an unlimited budget for reaching and making an impact on your buyer. What would you do if this were the case? Would you brand a hot-air balloon and fly it over your buyer's offices? Charter a jet to land on the roof of their headquarters and take them for lunch?

An unlimited budget is pretty unlikely, but it will do wonders in setting your mind racing with ideas.

Keep these wild ideas close and then scale back. What impact would that hot-air balloon make? Could you create that same impact with the budget you have? Or zero budget? How would you use the tools you already have to do this?

39

ACCESS THE

Feeler:

3 THINGS

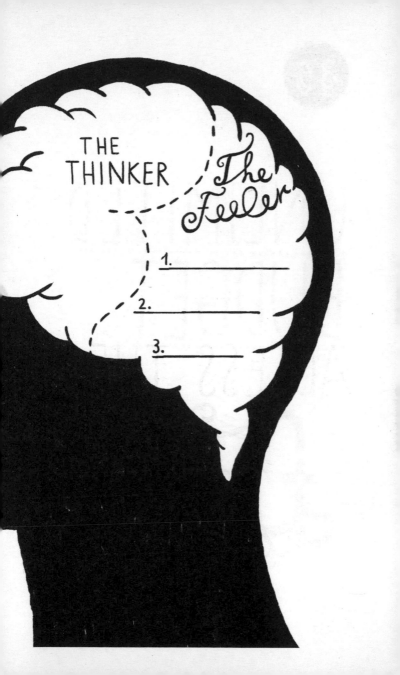

THE
THINKER

The Feeler

1. _____

2. _____

3. _____

UNLIMITED BUDGET

You'll find that by pushing your mind like this, you'll free yourself from self-inflicted mental restraints – and the path to the ideal solution will be far clearer.

TRY THIS:
What would you do if you had all the money in the world to excite your buyer? Write down all your wildest ideas. Now – what are the effects that you could replicate with a smaller budget, or none?

TOOL 41: WHAT'S NOW?

When inspiration is hard to find from within your market or product, look at what's going on in the media – what's a hot topic in the outside world that you could use to find connections and give your Thinker material to play with?

These hot topics can inform wonderful ideas to share with your buyer.

TRY THIS:
Look at what's 'now' in the media, in politics, in business, in life. Explore the current exciting trends in fashion, art, film or literature. What topics are capturing the public's imagination and how might you associate your project with this trend?

3. PONDER

Time is another wonderful aid to creative thinking. Giving your mind as long as possible to come up with something original, and learning to tolerate the discomfort of pondering and indecision, will provide you with astonishing results.

Interestingly, the creative process is one of the few activities where *not* being focused is more important than being focused. By allowing your mind to be in this state, you will find that your unconscious does the work and eventually sends your Thinker a message.

You need to take a step back and disengage your thoughts from critical attention. And you can't rush it.

This is where brainstorming often falls down; there is not enough time between the brief and the final idea. Brainstorms are great for getting everything on the table, but not for the development of ideas.

For this you need proper incubation time.

TOOL 42: FIND YOUR THIRD PLACE

Where do you have your best ideas? In the park? In a cafe? On the train? You can never predict where you'll have that 'aha!' moment. But it's rarely at home or at your desk. More pertinently, it's rarely in a place which characterises a high-stress environment.

Defining home as the 'first place' and the workplace as the 'second place', social psychologist Ray Oldenburg talks about the idea of a 'third place', where you can escape overly familiar surroundings and broaden your social experiences. Third places are where diverse talent has traditionally gathered to generate ideas, and they can be anywhere that is open and unpressured; your third place might be a beer garden, park, pub, cafe or post office. Anywhere where your mind can relax.

Your third place may be where you generate the majority of your ideas because of what are called 'alpha brain waves'. Many studies have revealed that insight is often generated following a burst of these brain waves; being able to generate them is the key to creative inspiration. Alpha brain waves were the first brain waves to be discovered by German neurologist Hans Berger in 1929 and are proven to be most present in a wakeful state of mind that is characterised by an effortless alertness. Essentially, when feeling relaxed, the brain works better.

Perhaps this is why my best ideas come just as I'm lying down for a snooze – just before I drop off to sleep, I get a rush of ideas.

42

FIND YOUR THIRD PLACE

WORK

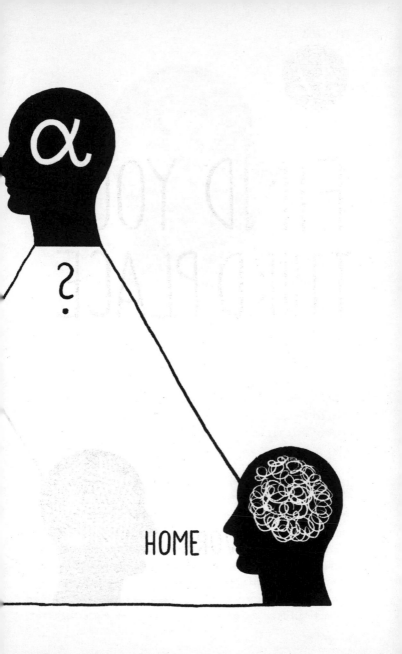

TRY THIS:

Identify a place where you are relaxed, and where you can let yourself idly ponder ideas, without feeling the pressure of committing them to memory. Think of an idea like a little mouse that needs to be coaxed out carefully.

Take your time. Don't try and solve your problem or brief right there and then. Let it percolate at the back of your mind as you go about your daily business and don't expect it to happen at your desk. Where is your third place? Wherever it is, seek it out when you need a rush of good ideas.

TOOL 43: UP THE TEMPO

Recent research has shown that walking can increase creative thought by up to 60 per cent. Geoff Nicholson, author of *The Lost Art of Walking*, believes in the importance of walking mindfully and without distractions: 'There is something about the pace of walking and the pace of thinking that goes together. Walking requires a certain amount of attention but it leaves great parts of the time open to thinking. I do believe once you get the blood flowing through the brain it does start working more creatively.' This makes walking the perfect activity to do while pondering a project.

Walking has long been cherished by writers working on their ideas. Charles Dickens was a walker, easily clocking up twenty miles a night. Wordsworth tramped the Lake District, Virginia Woolf, George Orwell and Friedrich Nietzsche all walked for inspiration.

The trick is to go out for a walk free of distractions. No headphones, no music, no audiobooks – leave your smartphone at home and give your mind time to have long thoughts, where you can play with ideas without interruption.

Up the tempo and run if that helps. Your blood will be pumping faster and you may feel more alert than when you just walk, certainly more awake than just sitting at your desk.

TRY THIS:
Put on your trainers and get out of the office. Go for a short walk around the block, or down the street. After work, you could try walking for longer – to the next bus stop, around a local park, or all the way home. Walk with no distractions, living in the moment. Your senses are sharpened and you can take in stimuli but work on the problem at the same time.

TOOL 44: LOOK UP

Historian Simon Schama recently said that we have become the 'look down' generation – we frequently lower our gaze to interact with our phone or tablet, rather than looking at the world around us. Schama thinks this is leading us to be more disconnected from the real world and from creativity.

In contrast a technique called 'dérive'– which means literally 'drift'– deliberately uses walking as a way to stimulate new and creative thoughts, by walking without purpose and observing the world around us.

43 Up t
Tempo

HOM

PARK

ENGLISH HERITAGE

HARRY
BECK
1902 - 1974
Designer of the London
Underground map

was born here

1008

*Look
Up*

Try looking up for a change. Inspiration can come from anywhere, and the most random places can reveal stimulating surprises. Marcel Proust used train timetables for inspiration, imagining what the towns at each stop were like, and who lived there. Try finding stimulus in the world around you and not just from Google.

TRY THIS:
Go out on the streets fully loaded with your problem and use what you see to formulate your solution. Notice everything. Perhaps a ladder could represent your buyer's challenges. Or a blue plaque could inspire the idea of visually representing how important your product is in its market.

THE 'AHA!' MOMENT

You have given your mind the brief, time, blood flow and inspiration. You have prepared for your idea, played with thoughts and pondered your problem. After all the time you've spent preparing, playing and pondering, the thinking brain is ready to receive a message from the Feeler: now is time for that 'aha!' moment.

TOOL 45: ACCESS THE FEELER: PENS AT THE READY

When your idea comes, it will be at the least expected moment, so be sure to have paper and pen handy at all times. You need to get the idea down on paper – if you don't, I guarantee that you will forget it.

TRY THIS:
Carry a pad with you at all times. Or use the notes function on your phone. Since ideas come at any moment and are not held in your consciousness for long, you need to get them written down. Bad ideas matter too; write it all down.

TOOL 46: THE REALITY SCALE

A problem with creative ideas is that they can sometimes be so wildly creative that they're not related to the buyer whatsoever. If you try to use them in your project, you'll fail to have any impact. Remember: like your effective interpretation, your ideas must spring from empathy with your buyer, and that means they must connect with your buyer's reality. Once you have written them down, try to rein them back to reality.

Look at the scale in Tool 46 – at one end is an idea that is utterly grounded in reality, an idea so rooted that it is, in fact, barely an idea and more of an observation. It's overly familiar and dull. At the other end of the scale is an idea that is way out there, totally untethered from reality, and incomprehensible and alienating for your buyer. In the middle is the sweet spot – this is where you want your idea to be. Not absurd, not boring, but exciting and relevant.

TRY THIS:
When you have had your idea, and written it down, give it time to breathe. Go back to it a few hours or even days later and think about how it relates to solving your buyer's problems. Is the idea close to their reality?

46

THE »REALITY« SCALE

GROUNDED IN YOUR
BUYER'S REALITY

RETHINK

Perfect

RETHINK

WAY OUT THERE

sing the Sale'

'HOWEVER BEAUTIFUL THE
STRATEGY, YOU SHOULD
OCCASIONALLY LOOK AT
THE RESULTS.'
WINSTON CHURCHILL

It would be difficult to write a book on selling without including a section on closing the deal, on generating that all-important and triumphant 'yes, please!' This is because, however thorough your activity throughout all the steps in the selling process, if you don't eventually secure the business, if the deal is ultimately left undone, then mastery of the skills will be somewhat pointless.

To sell is, in essence, to close, and to close today is to start closing right at the very beginning of your sell. It's a common misconception that the steps that lead to the 'yes, please' all happen at the end of the process.

This could not be further from the truth, for it's not at the end, nor mid-way through the sell that the seller must picture how to close. Ideally, you should be doing this right at the beginning, in that first conversation – whether over the phone, face-to-face or via the written word. And the effort must be continuous and spread across the entire process, not exerted all at the end.

Think about it like your years at university. Maybe you messed around in your first year, and the second year too, and pulled it all together in the third – but it wasn't quite enough to secure that first you so desired. In contrast, if you had diligently worked from day one, getting that high grade would have been infinitely easier. A steady effort is always going to make it easier to secure the desired outcome.

To effectively close the deal, to move a customer from cold to 'I get what these guys are about and I want some', takes a different approach to a pushy close.

You may consider closing to be a complex, opaque activity and success to be based on luck as much as skill. But, like the entire skill, it's actually incredibly simple.

To close the deal involves all skills of the entire **to see**, **to think** and **to improve**. The forty-eight tools in this book have all been designed to make the close achievable. And the following two tools are both a consolidation of previous lessons and offer a few extra activities that apply a healthy amount of psychological pressure. They are designed to enliven the hot buttons introduced in the PBI, and ultimately build trust.

TOOL 47: THE LADDER

I have identified as many as ten steps that must run through the entire sell to make the close as straightforward as possible. Think of it as a ladder – each rung is an important step towards reaching the summit. You could skip a rung or two, but no more. And you certainly can't jump straight to the top. The point is that the bulk of closing activity comes throughout the sell and should not be left to the end.

The ten steps incorporate some of the skills we've examined before and some are new here.

1. Recognise

At the beginning stages of any new prospect relationship, you must be alert to what it is that will generate the close.

After an initial chat, a call or a longer meeting, during which you have gathered the knowledge you need to move to the next stage, something will surface as your buyer's primary challenge or central goal. And your subsequent synthesis will identify how you'd position yourself to solve or support this.

Your solution should now sit at the centre of your communication with your prospect. You may well need to communicate on any

47

THE
LADDER

* Close *

THE HIGH ROAD	☐
AGITATE, DON'T IRRITATE	☐
SAY IT. DO IT.	☐
LITTLE YESES	☐
TASTE IT	☐
SHARE—ABILITY	☐
DON'T BE IKEA	☐
PRE-EMPT CHALLENGES	☐
THINK BIG PICTURE	☐
RECOGNISE	☐

number of topics, but this central theme should be reiterated as often as possible. Don't swerve too far from it. Focus on delivering it.

2. Think 'big picture'

A big mistake I witness time and again is sellers' failure to understand where their product fits in the grander scheme of things. Like in Tool 19, Think Big and Small, this is your buyer's B.

You're offering a daily news bulletin, let's say – but how is this going to help the company become No. 1 in its market? You're offering office refurbishment – but how is this going to make the prospect the most vibrant firm in their sector? You won't want to position yourself as solving these questions. But to close, you have to know the answers, you have to know B, and you have to be able to communicate them.

Knowledge of precisely how your product fits into, and contributes to, the bigger picture will help you build a stronger relationship with your prospect. Your communications must keep this central theme in mind.

3. Pre-empt challenges

Human relationships are fraught with difficulty – not just our personal relationships but our business ones too. Why are relationships so hard? Because we have different goals, agendas, pressures, anxieties and expectations. And to make this even more challenging, these change. The best closing recognises up-front the difficulties in working together.

The ABI helped us to recognise our buyer's anxieties and preconceived ideas. You can also recognise anxieties in your personal life – most frustrations, anger, anxiety and, in turn, arguments and break-ups, stem from these anxieties.

If you can recognise and anticipate the fears in the relationship with your buyer, then your relationship will be much more harmonious and successful.

From the beginning, try and think of their worst day and not their best, recognising what might put them off you, and tackle this head on. Include the solution to a situation that hasn't yet happened in your proposal. This will help you head off any negative ideas about your offer that might prevent the close.

Recently, a client of ours was pitching to a firm in Bristol, even though my client's business was based in London. Rather than hide this potential travel issue, my client addressed it head on, arranging weekly meetings at the prospect's HQ, bolstered by a weekly Skype session to keep everyone on track. By nipping the fear in the bud, you prevent it growing in significance.

4. Don't be Ikea
Nobody wants to invest in a product that will add to their workload. I see it all the time – some products take six months to integrate with your current systems, some need a week's induction to figure out how to use them, some consultancies want every last detail about the history of your firm and offer you no guidance on how to gather this. You get the picture: many firms start their sell by adding workload to their prospect's agenda, not taking it away.

Ikea offers cheap furniture that takes a day to build; it's bearable on a wet weekend but a no-no during a busy working week. We don't want the cheap, do-it-yourself product. We want the product that comes pre-made and made incredibly well – better than we could do it ourselves.

So don't be like Ikea. Instead, position yourself as the ready-made furniture store. Make it easy to buy from you and use you.

If you do need details about your client, make it really easy for them to give these to you, and include how you'll do this in your pitch. Or if it takes six months to integrate your software into their current infrastructure, then hold their hand every step of the way and tell them how you'll do this.

5. Share-ability

In any business there is often more than one decision-maker and as your communication is passed from one person to another the impact can be lost.

You know how it is: you meet Karen and Karen passes your communication to Peter, where it gets stuck and doesn't move for what seems like an eternity. Peter makes the decisions but you haven't met Peter. How can you expect him to trust and like you when all the good stuff was communicated in the face-to-face meeting with Karen?

The trick is to make sure that the follow-up communication is un-ignorable. Your pitch must ooze empathy, relevance and resonance. Think about what you've included in your sell. Have you de-chunked, made your hook clear, and used ethos, pathos and logos to present a clear argument? Use the check list below.

And why not remove any ambiguity in your story and have the first page as a visual to demonstrate precisely how you'll enhance their current situation? Use Tool 33, Draw It: Three Steps, to demonstrate precisely how you'll improve their status quo.

TOOL TICK LIST:	
DE-CHUNKED ?	☐
HOOK ?	☐
ETHOS, PATHOS, LOGOS ?	☐
STORY STAR ?	☐
HAVE YOU DRAWN IT ?	☐

6. Taste it

Almost every software system available on the market now offers buyers a demo experience. Not necessarily all are good demo experiences, but they offer a trial of the product none the less. And this is a crucial step on the closing-the-deal ladder.

In a climate bulging with competition, where a promise is no longer enough, a taster is much more attractive. Even firms that haven't historically been able to package their product to offer a demo need to figure out a way to do this.

Is there a way you can package your content? Could you offer a snippet of advice for free if your buyer tells you their needs? Could you create a quick tool that enables them to evaluate their own situation and get a score, or to benchmark themselves against competitors? This would be useful information and a great taster for your methods.

For a PR client, we suggested they offer to identify key influencers for their prospect's business. This was a hot topic in a PR market looking for new ways to get their content reviewed, shared and liked. To do this, our client ran a quick analysis on who was talking about the prospect firm and who they should be engaging with. The highly useful and unique data was shared and trust was forged. It was a brilliant 'taste-it' offer.

By creating powerful touch points – not pushy, just useful – you'll increase your chance of the 'yes, please'.

7. Little yeses
Closing can sometimes feel like a very long journey. It can be months, even years, from the initial meeting until you eventually get the sale. And this time isn't getting shorter; buying cycles are extending.

How do you keep your buyer close and engaged during this journey? The answer is little yeses all along the way.

It could be as simple as communicating:
You: 'Shall I summarise our discussions to date for you to share?'

Buyer: 'Yes, please.'

Or:
You: 'Let me analyse your language to give you a benchmark.'

Buyer: 'Yes, please.'

Or:
You: 'Let's chat again in September when things have settled for you and we can make a suitable plan.'

Buyer: 'Yes, please.'

Little yeses build reciprocity (see the PBI), trust and generally work to strengthen and differentiate your relationship with the buyer.

8. Say it. Do it

Obvious, right? You need to do everything you say you're going to do; don't make false promises. If you say you'll send a report, then send it. If you say you're going to get your colleague to get in touch to help with a problem, then make sure they get in touch.

A negative feeling lingers on in our mind much longer than a positive one. And we often don't even know why we have that negative feeling about that person or firm – it's an unconscious feeling, but powerful none the less. Not doing something that your buyer was expecting will definitely leave a negative memory in their mind.

Say it. Do it. A simple rule of thumb for sales, business and life.

9. Agitate, don't irritate

Whilst pushing to get the close is an absolute no-no, adding a sense of urgency can help your closing no end. This is the difference between irritation and agitation. Push and you'll lose, but keep them on their toes, keep them up to speed with who else has signed you up, how they are getting behind the curve or missing out on valuable insight, and you'll build desire nicely. This isn't a case of 'checking in', which is bound to irritate, but sharing something that is genuinely shareable and enticing.

Make your communication add urgency to the sell. Make it pressing, a no-brainer, but don't push.

10. Take the high road

We all have busy days, weeks, months when 'that' project doesn't even get a look in. Your buyer will be experiencing this too. When they met you, they got very excited and gave the impression they would have a sign-off for your service very quickly. But in reality, their day job, their life, health, family, economy – whatever it may be – is more immediate and more pressing. Stuff just gets in the way and things can take much longer than expected to come to fruition.

Don't think that because your email is left unopened it's because they don't like or want your product. Don't obsess about open rates and lack of response. They might genuinely be busy.

Take the high road with every sell and don't get dragged down by lack of response. Be the bigger person and recognise that life takes over. Sooner or later, you'll get that email you were waiting for.

Closed!

TRY THIS:
On the ladder, recognise the ten key steps to achieving the close. How could you implement any of the stages in your own scenario? They aren't necessarily in consecutive order; the more of them you use, the stronger your position will be, but the point is to use as many as you can throughout your sell rather than push for the close at the end.

TOOL 48: TASTE IT

This tool relates directly to Tool 8, The Passive Buyer Impression, and more specifically to the hot buttons of reciprocity, familiarity and likeability. We are more inclined to be persuaded by someone if we feel we owe them something, if they have given us something and we are propelled to repay them in some way. If we are actually given time to test the product, it will indeed become familiar. And of course, if we try it and like it, we're likely to proceed with the process. This concept is also included as a step in Tool 47, The Ladder.

So why is it so important to repeat this idea and create its own tool? Because, in a crowded market, in which one firm may offer the same benefit as multiple other firms, the only real way to differentiate is to demonstrate.

What would tempt
your buyer?

_____

Giving the buyer the chance to taste exactly how you'd work for them will set many of their hot buttons buzzing and do wonders to remove any hidden elements of your offer, reducing the risk and dissolving any fears and preconceived ideas.

Software firms are understandably keen on these demos. Some get it just right, whilst others have some work to do in making even the free demo experience appealing. But beyond these techie firms, almost any service can package their offer as a 'taste it'.

Examples
For a language-software client we developed a 'taste it' which enabled prospects to benchmark their language against the Millennials, a hugely influential age bracket.

For a leadership-development firm we created a digital tool which enabled the prospect to score their internal pressures and categorise themselves as a wounded, conservative or performance organisation. A very empathetic and useful 'taste it'.

Each of these examples enabled the buyer to test the experience and taste what it might be like if they ended up buying into a longer-term arrangement.

TRY THIS:
Identify what it is about your offer, related to your buyer's reality, that would work as a taster. Draw on your knowledge from the ABI, their bigger picture and future market trends.

What could you offer as a 'taster'? There is always something.

'Concluding Thoughts'

'THERE'S NOTHING NEW UNDER THE SUN. IT HAS ALL BEEN DONE BEFORE.'

SHERLOCK HOLMES

CONCLUDING THOUGHTS

In writing this book I wanted to highlight the brilliance of the human mind. It's a tool we all carry with us and can use to solve almost any challenge with which we're faced – including any sales challenge.

Our mind, with its inherent range of skills developed over thousands of years, skills which allow us to master the non-linear better than any machine and to have better ideas and more creative breakthroughs than any algorithm could muster – this is our ultimate tool in any sales scenario.

Yet our mind is subject to imperfections and limitations, and we are confronted every day by a host of challenges which prevent us performing at our best – from unstructured working lives and an overload of information, to our own egocentric bias. All cause us to fail at simple sales tasks.

Over the course of this book you will have discovered ways to overcome these challenges, methods to clear distractions and focus your mind, tools to help you see, think and improve every day, in every sales situation.

Seeking the observant, the empathetic, the process-oriented and the holistic self isn't easy, but it is achievable none the less. As you will have learnt, the trick is to approach these imperfections and limitations mindfully. In sales, we must look to the future with excitement and not anxiety; through mastering our entire skill, we become masters of ourselves and are able to sell more effectively.

The forty-eight tools in this book are designed to help you do just this. Allowing you to master each step of your sell, fully awake and personally in control.

THE TOOLS IN YOUR DAILY PRACTICE

Should you find yourself staring at a blank sheet of paper, struggling to see the light on a sales challenge, then one, a handful or maybe even all of these tools will help you focus your mind and guide you through the muddy waters of selling to reach the shore.

I'm sure, like most people who have used these tools, you'll have your favourites, and that's how I want it to be. Dip in, dip out – use some more than others but use them in your own scenarios and come to recognise and benefit from the selling experience that went into putting the tools together.

The cash value will come when, by using these ideas, you not only see improvement in your selling activity but find you're no longer stuck at any stage of your sell. You no longer draw a blank when fresh ideas are needed.

There is absolute power in mastery of your sales mind. Those sellers who can master a mindful approach to their selling and learn to switch it on when necessary will ultimately win.

You've got the sales mind – now go get the sale.

Good luck!

BIBLIOGRAPHY

In writing this book, I have not only looked to other sales writers for wisdom, but have drawn heavily from the shelves of advertising, psychology, neuroscience and even philosophy books. The writers in these genres explore their subjects in depth, and as such can provide a rich source of answers to our sales questions.

1. MEET YOUR SALES MIND

Books

Kurzweil, R., *The Singularity is Near*, Duckworth, 2006

Kurzweil, R., *How to Create a Mind*, Duckworth, 2014

Pinker, S., *The Language Instinct*, Penguin, 1994

Pinker, S., *How the Mind Works*, Penguin, 1997

Papers and Articles

Grothaus, M., 'The Top Jobs in 10 Years Might Not Be What You Expect', *Fast Company*, May 2015

Talks and Interviews

Sutherland, R., 'Perspective is everything', talk at TEDx Athens, December 2011

2. THE BRAIN: A SELLER'S GUIDE

Books

André, C., *Mindfulness: 25 Ways to Live in the Moment through Art*, Rider, 2014

Carter, R., *Mapping the Mind*, University of California Press, 2010, first published 1998

Chatfield, T., *How to Thrive in the Digital Age*, The School of Life, Macmillan, 2012

De Botton, A., *The Consolations of Philosophy*, Penguin, 2001

Edwards, B., *Drawing on the Right Side of the Brain*, HarperCollins, 2008, first published 1979

James, W., *The Energies of Men*, Moffat, Yard and Company, 1907

Jarrett, C., *The Rough Guide to Psychology*, Rough Guides, 2011

Kahneman, D., *Thinking Fast and Slow*, Penguin, 2011

Kosslyn, S. M. and Miller, W. D., *Top Brain, Bottom Brain: Surprising Insights into How You Think*, Simon & Schuster, 2013

Langer, E. J., *Mindfulness*, Perseus Books, 1989

Linden, D., *The Accidental Mind*, Harvard University Press, 2008

McManus, C., *Right Hand, Left Hand*, Phoenix, 2003, first published by Weidenfeld and Nicolson, 2002

Pink, D. H., *A Whole New Mind: Why Right Brainers Will Rule the Future*, Penguin, 2008, first published by Riverhead Books, 2005

Pinker, S., *How the Mind Works*, Penguin, 1997

Snowden, R., *Jung: The Key Ideas*, Hodder Education, 2006

Papers and Articles

Killingsworth M. A. and Gilbert, D. T., 'Wandering Mind not a Happy Mind', *Harvard Gazette*, November 2010

Mark, G., Gonzalez, V. M., Harris, J., 'The Cost of Interrupted Work: More Speed and Stress', Proceedings of the SIGCHI conference on Human Factors in Computing Systems, 2008

Miller, G. A., 'The Magical Number Seven, Plus or Minus Two: Some Limits on Our Capacity for Processing Information', *Psychological Review*, 1956

Talks and Interviews

Daisley, B., interview in November 2014

Lavie, N., interview in February 2015

3. THE SELLER MINDSHIFT

Books

Allen, D., *Getting Things Done: The Art of Stress-free Productivity*, Penguin, 2002

Foley, M., *Life Lessons from Bergson*, The School of Life, Macmillan, 2013

James, W., *Talk to Teachers on Psychology*, H. Holt, 1900

Langer, E. J., *Mindfulness*, Perseus Books, 1989

Michalko, M., *Thinkertoys*, Ten Speed Press, 2006, first published 1991

Papers and Articles

Lohr, S., 'Slow Down, Brave Multitasker, and Don't Read This in Traffic', *New York Times*, March 2007

Talks and Interviews

Lavie, N., interview in February 2015

4. TO SEE

Books

Burnett, L., in D. Higgins, *The Art of Writing Advertising: Conversations with Masters of the Craft*, NTC Business Books, 1965

Cialdini, R. B., *Influence: The Psychology of Persuasion*, HarperCollins, 2007

Dixon, M., Adamson, B., *The Challenger Sale: Taking Control of the Customer Conversation*, Penguin, 2013

Hopkins, C., *My Life in Advertising and Scientific Advertising*, McGraw Hill, 1986, first published by Crain Communications 1966

LaBarre, P. and Taylor, C. W., *Mavericks at Work: Why the Most Original Minds in Business Win*, HarperCollins, 2008, first published 2006

Lamott, A., *Bird by Bird: Instructions on Writing and Life*, Anchor Books, 1995

Langer, E. J., *Mindfulness*, Perseus Books, 1989

Morgan, A., *The Pirate Inside: Building a Challenger Brand Culture Within Yourself and Your Organizations*, Wiley, 2004

Ogilvy, D., *Ogilvy on Advertising*, Prion, 2011, first published by Pan Books and Orbis Publishing, 1983

Taleb, N., *The Black Swan: The Impact of the Highly Improbable*, Random House, 2010, first published 2007

Papers and Articles

Maslow, A. H., 'A Theory of Human Motivation', *Psychological Review*, 1943

Talks and Interviews

Miller, G. A., 'The Magical Number Seven, Plus or Minus Two: Some Limits on Our Capacity for Processing Information', *Psychological Review*, 1956

Messett, T., interview in August 2014

5. TO THINK

Books

Allen, D., *Getting Things Done: The Art of Stress-free Productivity*, Penguin, 2002

Bergson, H., *Key Writings*, Continuum, 2002

Bernbach, W. and Burnett, L., in D. Higgins, *The Art of Writing Advertising: Conversations with Masters of the Craft*, NTC Business Books, 1965

Buster, B., *Do Story: How to Tell Your Story so the World Listens*, The Do Book Company, 2013

Conrad, B., Schulz, M. *Snoopy's Guide to the Writing Life*, Writer's Digest Books, 2002

Fonagy, P., Gergely, G., Jurist, E. L., *Affect Regulation, Mentalisation and the Development of the Self*, Karnac, 2004

Gardner, H., *Frames of Mind: The Theory of Multiple Intelligences*, Basic Books, 1993, first published 1983

Gross, C. G., *Brain, Vision, Memory: Tales in the History of Neuroscience*, MIT Press, 1999

Jenkins, D. and Sommers, C., *Whiteboard Selling: Empowering through Visuals*, Wiley, 2013

Kipling, R., *The Elephant's Child*, Francis Lincoln Books, 2007, first published 1902

Lehrer, J., *Proust was a Neuroscientist*, Houghton Mifflin Books, 2007

Ogilvy, D., *Ogilvy on Advertising*, Prion, 2011, first published by Pan Books and Orbis Publishing, 1983

Perry, P., *How to Stay Sane*, The School of Life, Macmillan, 2012

Pinker, S., *The Sense of Style: The Thinking Person's Guide to Writing in the 21st Century*, Penguin, 2014

Roam, D., *The Back of the Napkin: Solving Problems and Selling Ideas with Pictures*, Marshall Cavendish Business, 2009

Papers and Articles
Ambady, N., Rosenthal, R., 'Thin Slices of Expressive Behavior as Predictors of Interpersonal Consequences: A Meta-analysis', *Psychological Bulletin*, 1992

Shepard, R. N., 'Recognition Memory for Words, Sentences, and Pictures', *Journal of Learning and Verbal Behavior*, 1967

Talks and Interviews
Daisley, B., interview in November 2014

6. TO IMPROVE

Books
Carey, B., *How We Learn: The Surprising Truth about When, Where and Why it Happens*, Random House, 2014

De Botton, A., *How Proust Can Change Your Life*, Picador, 1997

Dennett, D. C., *Intuition Pumps and Other Tools for Thinking*, Penguin, 2014

Gardner, H., *Five Minds for the Future*, Harvard Business School Press, 2006

Hopkins, C., *My Life in Advertising and Scientific Advertising*, McGraw Hill, 1986, first published by Crain Communications 1966

Langer, E. J., *Mindfulness*, Perseus Books, 1989

James, W., *Essays in Psychology*, Harvard University Press, 1983

Ogilvy, D., *Ogilvy on Advertising*, Prion, 2011, first published by Pan Books and Orbis Publishing, 1983

Nicholson, G., *The Lost Art of Walking: The History, Science, Philosophy, Literature, Theory and Practice of Pedestrianism*, Riverhead Books, 2008

Oldenburg, R., *Celebrating the Third Place: Inspiring Stories about the 'Great Good Places' at the Heart of Our Communities*, Marlowe & Company, 2002

Skinner, B. F., *The Behavior of Organisms*, D. Appleton & Company, 1938

Papers and Articles

Greenfield, R., 'How Disney's Imagineers Keep the Magic Ideas Coming: Interview with Peter Rummell', *Fast Company*, 2014

FURTHER READING

All of Kevin Duncan's books are useful, particularly *The Diagrams Book*.

New Scientist magazine is well worth a subscription – it's filled with the latest research on the human mind.

Modern marketing wouldn't be the same without Seth Godin.

Dave Trott provides a no-nonsense take on everything and anything related to business and creativity.

For a contemporary look at creativity in the workplace, Chris Barez is great.

ACKNOWLEDGEMENTS

Help, motivational support and advice came from various quarters. Big thanks to: Tim for his brilliant daddying, which freed up time to consolidate disparate thoughts into a book; Kat Leuzinger, an illustrator in a million and a brilliantly talented lady – I hugely value her work and our blossoming friendship; everyone at Profile Books who has worked tirelessly to create this piece of my life, especially Clare Grist Taylor for her enthusiasm and sound judgement all along this journey, and Louisa Dunnigan whose attention to detail, patience and organisational talents are a lesson to us all; Jasmine Naim, Alex Rickerby, Kevin Duncan and my dear school friends for their encouragement along the way; and Nilli Lavie, Bruce Daisley and Thomas Messett for the rich insight they shared in the early days of research for the book.

Last but not least to my mother for passing on her natural ability to sell anything to anyone which provided the ideal early learning ground – and for that I'm truly grateful.

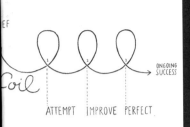

ongoing success

ATTEMPT IMPROVE PERFECT

The Reality Check

LIFE

time

GET PHYSICAL

PRODUCT FEATURE

e.g. Twitter Monitoring

CONCRETE LANGUAGE

e.g. we collect and count clicks

Up the tempo

HOME

MOUNTAIN

WORK

ABI {PERSONAL}

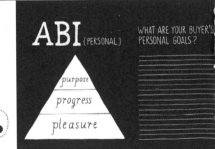

purpose

progress

pleasure

WHAT ARE YOUR BUYER'S PERSONAL GOALS?

Buyer

THE KILLER SUBJECT LINE

MAIL MESSAGE

SEND SAVE DELETE

TO

SUBJECT: